BIRNBAUM GUIDES

2008

Walt Disney World®

For KIDS

Wendy Lefkon
Editorial Director

Jill Safro
Editor

Debbie Lofaso
Designer

Jessica Ward
Editorial Assistant

Jody Revenson
Consulting Editor

Alexandra Mayes Birnbaum
Consulting Editor

THE OFFICIAL GUIDE

DISNEP EDITIONS

ISBN-13: 978-1-4321-0387-5
ISBN-10: 1-4321-0387-4

Printed in the United States of America

An enormous debt of gratitude is owed to Dave Herbst, Laura Simpson,
Darlene Papalini, Craig Dezern, Debbie Dizon, Kristi Koester, Jay Zavada, Bebee Frost,
Jen Marsico, Pattie Loepper, Leonard Erb, Marilyn Erb, Natalie Johnson, Jim Oliver,
Stacey Cook, Irene Ferdinand, Jeff Titelius, Amy Safro, and Frieda Christofides, all of whom
performed above and beyond the call of duty to make the creation of this book possible. And
to Phil Lengyel, Tom Elrod, Linda Warren, Bob Miller, and Charlie Ridgway, thanks for believ-
ing in this project in the first place.

Other 2008 Birnbaum's Official Disney Guides

Disney Cruise Line
Disney Dining
Disneyland
Walt Disney World
Walt Disney World Without Kids

CONTENTS

You're Going to Disney World!

When you first heard the news, you couldn't believe your ears. Could it be true? Were you really going on a vacation to Walt Disney World? Well, believe it or not, it's true! Before you know it, you'll be in the sunny state of Florida. It's the home of Walt Disney World and the most famous mouse on planet Earth. (Hint: His name starts with *M*.)

If you have ever been there, you already know that it's one mighty big place with lots to do. In fact, there is so much going on that it can get a little confusing. That's where this book comes in handy. It describes everything in the World, from the Magic Kingdom theme park to the Hoop-Dee-Doo Musical Revue. And it's filled with advice from kids like you.

There is no right or wrong way to read this book. You can start on the first page and read straight through to the end. Or you can skip around, read your favorite parts first, and come back to the rest later.

No matter what you do, one thing is for sure: When you're done, you will be a true-blue Disney expert. Soon kids may start asking *you* for advice on how to have the most awesome vacation at Walt Disney World!

Pack a Pen and
Take Me Along With You!

Don't leave this book behind when you head for the parks. It's full of tips and opinions that you'll want to remember. There are pages for autographs, too—so don't forget to bring a pen. Here are some ways to use this book while visiting the wonderful world of Disney:

Track Your Trip

Each time you check out an attraction, check it off in this book. Then you'll know what's left to see on your next visit.

Search for Hidden Mickeys

Disney Imagineers have hidden images of Mickey all over Walt Disney World. (Many look like the three connected circles that form Mickey's head.) You might see them in shadows, lights, drawings, or even in the clouds at some attractions. Look in this book for each **Hidden Mickey Alert!** to find a Hidden Mickey clue. Keep track of the number of Hidden Mickeys that you discover. That way when the trip is over, you can write your findings on page 143 of this book's Magical Memories section.

Find the Fastpass

DISNEY'S FASTPASS

Would you like to walk right up to the front of the line at some of the most popular rides? What? Cut the line? Yes, you sure can—if you have a Fastpass in your hand. You can get one for any ride that has a Fastpass symbol by its name in this book. Here's how it works: You get a ticket from the ride's Fastpass machine. It tells you when to come back. Then, return at that time, and in just a few minutes you'll be on the ride! (Fastpass is free for all guests—as long as they have a valid park ticket.)

We're Warning You!

Disney rides are full of surprises. That's part of what makes them so much fun. But not everyone likes surprises. So if things like loud noises or fast turns scare you, look at the book's **attraction reaction** warnings before you go on each ride. That way, the only surprises you come across will be good ones!

The last pages of this book are for autographs.

What do the kids who helped with this book all have in common? They love Walt Disney World! How do we know? They told us so! Every kid who wrote to us last year received a survey form to fill out. These surveys came back filled with all different opinions about Walt Disney World. The forms also helped us find out about readers' interests and backgrounds.

What did we learn? For starters, a whole lot of you enjoy reading, writing, playing sports, drawing, and surfing the Internet. You also like dancing, singing, and making music. Your favorite place to stay at WDW is the Caribbean Beach resort. You're not crazy about loud rides. But thrill rides like Splash Mountain and Space Mountain are at the top of your list. You think Blizzard Beach is the perfect place to spend the day splashing around. And when you can't find a Mickey Mouse Ice Cream Bar to snack on, you love popcorn and chocolate chip cookies. Yum!

To everyone who filled out a survey, THANK YOU! This book couldn't have been written without you.

Jill Safro

Jill Safro
Editor

Mickey Is Number One!

It's probably not a surprise to hear that Mickey Mouse is still the most popular Disney character with readers. But who would've guessed that Minnie would be a close second? Rounding out the top five faves are Goofy, Donald Duck, and Tinker Bell. Who's your favorite? Let us know!

The Magic Kingdom Rules!

This year more than half of our readers picked the Magic Kingdom as their favorite theme park. Is it yours?

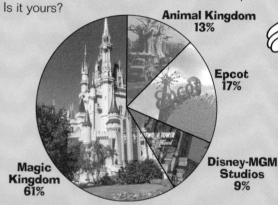

Animal Kingdom 13%

Epcot 17%

Disney-MGM Studios 9%

Magic Kingdom 61%

60%
50%
40%
35%
30%
25%
20%
15%
10%
5%
0%

Rough   Funny   Wet   Scary   Dark

You Have No Fear!

We asked you what types of rides you like best. It turns out most of you like the twists and turns of thrill rides. What daredevils!

Look for this Reader Pleaser ribbon throughout the book. We've placed it beside our readers' favorite Disney attractions, theme parks, snacks, and more. If you'd like to cast your vote for next year's Reader Pleasers, write us a letter and we'll send you a survey form. Our address is listed below.

The Reader Review

Every reader who was mailed a survey also got an application to become a Birnbaum Ace Reporter. The winning reviews appear at the end of many attractions in this book. Use the opinions of the Ace Reporters to decide if the ride is worth the wait or one to skip!

And the Winner is...

One lucky Ace Reporter was picked at random to win a special Disney prize. And the winner is . . . Jessilyn from Billings, Montana!

Jessilyn's favorite Walt Disney World attractions are Expedition Everest and Tower of Terror. Who's on top of her favorite character list? That would be Tinker Bell and Simba. She loves to read and write, play sports (expecially cross country running!), and have fun with family and friends.

Way to go, Jessilyn! And thanks for your input to this year's edition of "Walt Disney World For Kids."

READER TIP

Keep an eye out for this symbol. Every time you spot it, you'll find a great tip sent in by a reader. Do you have any Walt Disney World tips? We would love to hear them!

What do YOU think?

Do you agree or disagree with any of the kids in this book? Tell us! Send us a letter about your trip and a self-addressed, stamped envelope to us at the address on the right.

We will send you a survey, and read every letter before we write next year's book.

Birnbaum's Disney Guides
Kid Expert Applications
Disney Editions
114 Fifth Avenue, 14th Floor
New York, NY 10011

Meet the Editor

PHOTO BY GENE DUNCAN

Hi. My name's Jill. I'm one of the big kids who helped put this book together. (Mickey helped us out, too!)

Meet Walt Disney

Walt thought of Mickey as his own son.

Walt Disney was born in Illinois on December 5, 1901—that's more than one hundred years ago! During his life and for all the years after, Walt Disney's company created famous cartoons, movies, theme parks, books, and toys (plus much, much more) for everyone to enjoy . . . but how did it all begin?

When Walt was a little boy, he would look up at the sky and imagine the clouds were animals. As the wind pushed a cloud, a pig would turn into a cow. Soon, the cow would become a chicken! It was then that Walt realized that anything was possible with a little imagination.

But he knew that success would not come from daydreaming alone. Growing up on a farm had taught him the importance of hard work. And it's a good thing, because without Walt's hard work we would never have met the most famous mouse in the world.

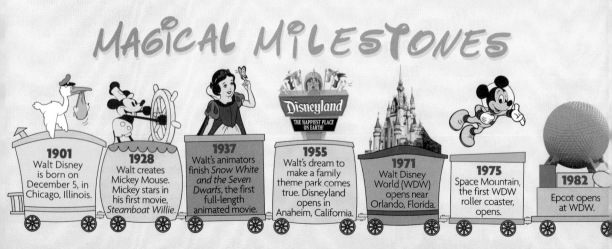

MAGICAL MILESTONES

1901 Walt Disney is born on December 5, in Chicago, Illinois.

1928 Walt creates Mickey Mouse. Mickey stars in his first movie, *Steamboat Willie*.

1937 Walt's animators finish *Snow White and the Seven Dwarfs*, the first full-length animated movie.

1955 Walt's dream to make a family theme park comes true. Disneyland opens in Anaheim, California.

1971 Walt Disney World (WDW) opens near Orlando, Florida.

1975 Space Mountain, the first WDW roller coaster, opens.

1982 Epcot opens at WDW.

A mouse is born

In 1928, Walt created a little cartoon mouse (who he almost named Mortimer Mouse. Luckily, Lilly Disney convinced her husband to name him Mickey Mouse instead!). Mickey's first movie was a black-and-white cartoon called *Steamboat Willie*. It was an instant success. But one hit wasn't enough for its creator. Walt was always looking for new challenges. In 1937, his animation company made the first full-length cartoon movie: *Snow White and the Seven Dwarfs*. Walt was very proud that he had made a movie for everyone in the family to enjoy.

Steamboat Willie was the first talking cartoon ever made.

Family was very important to Walt. Every Saturday, he would do something special with his two daughters. They often went to amusement parks. The kids loved it, but Walt was sad that there weren't rides for parents. *I wish there were a place where children and grown-ups could have fun together*, he thought.

Mickey looks pretty good for his age, doesn't he?

A dream is a wish your heart makes

Since a place like that didn't exist, Walt decided to build it. At first he was going to call it Mickey Mouse Park, but then he named it Disneyland. Disneyland opened in Anaheim, California, in 1955. Families traveled from all over the world to visit it. Disneyland was so popular that Walt's new dream was to build an even bigger park: Disney World. He must have wished upon a star—because his dream came true.

1983
Tokyo Disneyland opens in the capital city of Japan.

1989
Disney-MGM Studios opens at WDW.

1992
Disneyland Paris opens in France.

1996
WDW celebrates its 25th anniversary.

1998
Disney's Animal Kingdom opens at WDW.

2006
Expedition Everest opens in Animal Kingdom.

2007

Toy Story Mania opens at the Disney-MGM Studios.

What a Wonderful World

Walt Disney loved dreaming up stories to tell and new ways to tell them. After he died, his brother Roy kept one of his biggest dreams alive. He made sure Walt's special "world" was built just the way Walt had imagined it. Roy even insisted that it be called *Walt* Disney World, so everyone would know it had been his brother's dream.

Walt Disney World officially opened on October 1, 1971. Since then, millions of people have stopped in for a visit. Some people come to Walt Disney World for a day, but most stay a little longer. There's just so much to see and do.

Pick a theme park, any theme park

The most famous part of Walt Disney World is the **Magic Kingdom**. It's home to Cinderella Castle, Space Mountain, and those rascally Pirates of the Caribbean. It's also where Mickey, Minnie, and their pals keep their country cottages. Kids of all ages can't get enough of this happy place. Of course, there are three other theme parks to see.

Epcot is a place of science and discovery. Here you can search for Nemo at The Seas with Nemo and Friends. It's also a great place to go on a "world tour" or soar over California. Different countries have shops, restaurants, and attractions inside this park. Epcot opened in 1982.

Are you a showbiz fan? If so, you'll get a kick out of the **Disney-MGM Studios** theme park. It's filled with movie- and TV-themed rides and exhibits. The secrets of

animation are revealed at The Magic of Disney Animation. Belle and Gaston sing and dance at Beauty and the Beast—Live on Stage. And The Twilight Zone Tower of Terror scares *everybody* silly. The Disney-MGM Studios opened in 1989.

Disney's Animal Kingdom celebrates the wonders of nature and the creatures that live in it. It got off to a roaring start in 1998. The park has what it takes to make any kid's day: an African safari ride filled with wild animals, life-like dinosaurs, a roller coaster adventure with a scary abominable snowman, and a super slimy 3-D movie about bugs.

Chill out!

Need to cool off on a hot day? You can make a splash at a Disney water park. Between **Typhoon Lagoon** and **Blizzard Beach**, it's almost impossible to stay dry. Each one has slippery slides, tube rides, and some very cool pools.

But wait—there's more! Walt Disney World also has boats, bikes, and even horses to ride. It has hundreds of restaurants, shops, and other places to explore. In fact, no matter how many times you visit, there's always something new to see. Will Walt Disney World ever be finished? Not as long as there is imagination left in the world. And that's exactly how Walt would have wanted it.

Getting Ready to Go

Planning a vacation to Walt Disney World is lots of fun. But it's not as easy as it sounds. There are so many choices to make! Which parks should you visit? What should you pack? And where can you meet your favorite Disney characters? Use this book to answer these questions and help plan your family's vacation. Remember: It's never too early to get started!

Make a Simple Schedule

Did you know that there are more than 300 attractions at Walt Disney World? It could take weeks to see them all. And most people don't have weeks to spend on vacation! That's why it's important to make a schedule before you leave home. Without it, you might miss some of the rides you want to try the most.

What You'll Need
● Paper ● Pencil ● This book

What to Do

1. Write "Magic Kingdom" on the top of a piece of paper.

2. Look at the Magic Kingdom chapter. Every time you see an attraction that sounds like fun, write its name on the paper.

3. When you have finished the chapter, look over your list. Then put a star next to your ten favorite attractions. These are your "must-sees."

4. Now make a schedule for each of the other theme parks you plan to visit.

5. Don't forget to take your Simple Schedules to the parks!

Learn the Disney Lingo

Audio-Animatronics — Life-like robots, from birds and dinosaurs to movie stars and presidents. They seem real—but they're not.

Cast Member — A Disney employee.

Circle-Vision 360 — A movie that surrounds you. The screens form a circle.

Guidemap — A theme park map that also describes attractions, shops, restaurants, and entertainment.

Imagineer — A creative person who designs Disney attractions.

Save Room for Souvenirs

When you pack for your trip, make sure you're prepared for the weather. Believe it or not, it gets chilly in Florida, especially in the winter. But during the summer it's sizzling hot! It's usually warm during the rest of the year. Layers are a good idea, so you can take something off if you get hot. Remember to pack clothes and shoes that are lightweight and comfortable— since you'll do a lot of walking at the parks. And don't overstuff your suitcase. You'll need room for all the goodies you get at Walt Disney World.

What else should you bring? That's up to you! Here's a short list to help you get started:

- **A sweatshirt or sweater**
- **Broken-in sneakers or shoes**
- **Shorts and pants**
- **Long-sleeved and short-sleeved shirts**
- **A hat and sunglasses**
- **A bathing suit**
- **Sunscreen**

Visit Disney on the Internet

This book is chock-full of information about Disney, but there is another great place to learn about Walt Disney World: the Internet. Visit WDW's website at *www.disneyworld.com*.

If you have a question, send an e-mail, and you will get an answer in a few days. If you have a question and don't have access to the Internet, write to:

**Walt Disney World
Box 10000
Lake Buena Vista, FL 32830**

COUNTDOWN
TO WALT DISNEY WORLD

10

Start to plan a Disney dinner party. Select favorite vacation foods like hot dogs and ice cream for the menu. Who is on your guest list?

_____

_____

_____

9 DAYS 'TIL DISNEY

Get to work on your Magic Kingdom Simple Schedule. (Read page 12 to learn how.)

Which ride are you going to go on first?

_____

6

Make some Mouse ears—tape strips of paper together to make a loop big enough to fit around your head. Then cut out two circles and tape them to the front of the loop. Make a pair for everyone invited to your party.

5 MORE DAYS

Plan your Disney-MGM Studios Simple Schedule. The first two should be almost done by now!

And start packing! (Flip to page 13 for some packing tips.)

2 DAYS TO GO!

It's party time! Set the table to look festive for your special Disney dinner party. After dessert, share your theme park schedules with your family. Remember to wear your Mouse ears!

1 DAY LEFT

Don't stay up too late—tomorrow is the big day!

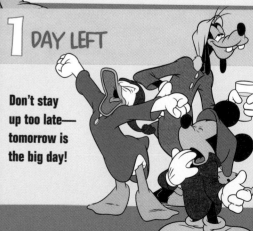

Take a look at a calendar. On which day does your Walt Disney World vacation begin? Once you find it, count back ten days—that's the day you can start this special countdown.

To do it, simply color in the number for each day as it arrives. Then try the daily activity. You can make up your own special activities, too!

8 DAYS LEFT

Make a list with the address of everyone you want to send a postcard to. (Don't forget about e-mail addresses for Internet postcards, too!)

7

It's time to start your Epcot Simple Schedule. Have you finished your Magic Kingdom schedule yet?

Which Epcot ride do you think sounds best? _____

4 DAYS

Pop some popcorn and watch your favorite Disney movie with your family.

Which flick did you pick?

_____

3

Spend some time on your Animal Kingdom Simple Schedule tonight. Finish up schedules for the other parks, too. Which theme park are you going to visit first?_____

You're going to Walt Disney World! Today's the day:

MONTH/DAY/YEAR

Magic Kingdom

READER
Favorite
Theme
Park
PLEASER

When most people hear the words "Walt Disney World," they think of Cinderella Castle, Space Mountain, and, of course, Mickey Mouse. They are all here in the Magic Kingdom, along with much more. That's why so many kids say the Magic Kingdom is the most special part of the World.

You can spend lots of time in its seven lands—Main Street, U.S.A., Adventureland, Frontierland, Liberty Square, Fantasyland, Mickey's Toontown Fair, and Tomorrowland. This chapter will help you decide which attractions you want to see first. Then flip back to page 12. It has tips on how to make a simple Magic Kingdom schedule. That way you can organize your visit and avoid wasting valuable time.

LIBERTY SQUARE
16 The Hall of Presidents
17 The Haunted Mansion
18 Liberty Belle Riverboat

FANTASYLAND
19 Cinderella's Golden Carrousel
20 Dumbo the Flying Elephant
21 It's a Small World
22 Mad Tea Party
23 The Many Adventures of Winnie the Pooh
24 Peter Pan's Flight
25 Mickey's PhilharMagic
26 Snow White's Scary Adventures
27 Ariel's Grotto

MICKEY'S TOONTOWN FAIR
28 Donald's Boat
29 Mickey's Country House
30 Minnie's Country House
31 Toontown Hall of Fame
32 The Barnstormer
33 Walt Disney World Railroad Station

TOMORROWLAND
34 Astro Orbiter
35 Buzz Lightyear's Space Ranger Spin
36 Stitch's Great Escape!
37 Tomorrowland Indy Speedway
38 Space Mountain
39 Tomorrowland Transit Authority
40 Monster's Inc.–The Laugh Floor

MAIN STREET, U.S.A.
1 Main Street Vehicles
2 Walt Disney World Railroad
3 Main Street Exposition Hall

ADVENTURELAND
4 Jungle Cruise
5 Pirates of the Caribbean
6 Swiss Family Treehouse
7 The Enchanted Tiki Room– Under New Management
8 The Magic Carpets of Aladdin

FRONTIERLAND
9 Big Thunder Mountain Railroad
10 Country Bear Jamboree
11 Frontierland Shootin' Arcade
12 Splash Mountain
13 Tom Sawyer Island
14 Diamond Horseshoe
15 Walt Disney World Railroad Station

········· Parade Route

You can get a bigger map of the Magic Kingdom at the park. It's free!

17

Main Street, U.S.A.

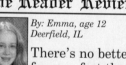

Are you ready for some time traveling? You'll do a lot of it in the Magic Kingdom. Four out of its seven lands send you either back or forward in time.

Main Street, U.S.A., is one of those lands. It was made to look like a small American town in the year 1900. (Some of it is based on the town Walt Disney grew up in—Marceline, Missouri.)

There are pretty lampposts, horse-drawn trolleys, and many other touches that make the street charming. If you look both ways before crossing, you'll notice a big difference between this Main Street and a real one: There's a castle at the end of it!

There are no major attractions here, but Main Street is a fun place to be. You can sink your teeth into a fresh-baked cookie, hop aboard a train, or watch a parade go by.

READER TIP

"The stores on Main Street stay open after the rest of the park closes!"

Greta (age 11)
Brewster, MA

The Reader Review

By: Emma, age 12
Deerfield, IL

There's no better cure for sore feet than a trip on the Walt Disney World Railroad. A friendly voice provides information about the park and there is a nice breeze. It's great for all ages.

Walt Disney World Railroad

Walt Disney loved trains. He even had a miniature one in his backyard that was big enough for him to ride on.

The Magic Kingdom trains are real locomotives that were built nearly a hundred years ago. A full trip takes about 20 minutes, but you can get on or off at any station (at Main Street, U.S.A., Frontierland, or Mickey's Toontown Fair).

What do most kids think about the Magic Kingdom's railroad? They love traveling by train. You get a great view of the park—plus a chance to rest your feet.

Play VMK!

The Main Street Cinema is VMK Central. What's VMK? The letters stand for Virtual Magic Kingdom—a free online game that lets kids create characters, play games, mix music, and more. You can play by getting your parents' permission and visiting *www.vmk.com*. Collect VMK rewards and maybe even go on a VMK Quest (a special scavenger hunt in the Magic Kingdom).

Main Street Vehicles

The Walt Disney World Railroad isn't the only transportation on Main Street, U.S.A. Horse-drawn trolleys, old-fashioned cars, and an antique fire engine make trips up and down the street throughout the day.

You can climb aboard any one of these vehicles in Town Square or by Cinderella Castle. Each trip is strictly one-way—you'll be asked to hop off after the ride.

The vehicles don't operate every day. Stop by City Hall (it's on Main Street) to find out when they are running.

When the horses that pull the trolleys are taking a break, you'll usually find them in the Car Barn near the Emporium. Drop in for a visit.

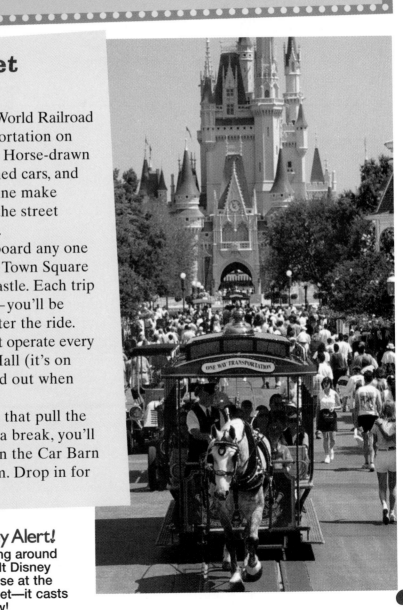

Hidden Mickey Alert!
Look by the railing around the statue of Walt Disney and Mickey Mouse at the end of Main Street—it casts a Mickey shadow!

Adventureland

A trip to Adventureland is like a visit to a tropical island. It has so many plants and trees that George of the Jungle would feel right at home. (Don't bother looking for him. He prefers his own treehouse to the one here. Besides, he probably couldn't find it if he tried.)

As you can tell from the name of this land, the attractions take you on exciting (and silly) adventures.

Hidden Mickey Alert!
As you enter Adventureland, look at the shields above the bridge. One has a Mickey head carved into it.

Jungle Cruise

It's a good thing elephants aren't shy. Otherwise, they might get upset when you watch them take a bath. That's just one of the interesting sights on the Jungle Cruise.

The voyage goes through the jungles of Africa and Asia. Along the way you see life-like zebras, giraffes, lions, hippos, and a few headhunters. (Don't worry—the only real animals in the ride are the humans inside the boat!)

The Jungle Cruise is usually very crowded—try to get there early in the morning. It's a good idea to ride during the day, when you can see everything. But if you want a spookier ride, take the cruise at night.

The Reader Review

By: Shawn, age 12
York, PA

I like this ride because of all the corny jokes the captain tells. They're so funny! I liked the animals better when I was younger, but I still ride to hear those famous jokes!

Hidden Mickey Alert!
Keep an eye out for the bathing elephants—a Mickey is carved into the rock behind them.

Magic Kingdom

PHOTO BY JILL SAFRO

HoT TiP

Are you a fan of the Pirates of the Caribbean movies? If so, you'll like the new pirates who have moved in at this attraction—keep your eyes peeled for Captain Barbossa and Captain Jack Sparrow!

Pirates of the Caribbean

Dead men tell no tales! That's the warning a pirate gives near the start of this attraction. Don't worry—this classic ride isn't going to hurt you. But there is a small dip and some dark scenes, so be prepared.

The journey takes place in a little boat. After floating through a cave ... *BOOM!* You're in the middle of a pirate attack! Cannons blast while the song "Yo Ho, Yo Ho, a Pirate's Life for Me" plays in the background.

Some of the pirates and animals look real. (They're actually Audio-Animatronics figures.) Halfway through the ride, look for a pirate with his leg hanging over a bridge—the leg is really hairy.

In case you didn't know: This is the attraction that inspired Disney's *Pirates of the Caribbean* movies. *Arrrrrr!*

The Reader Review

By: Jordan, age 12
Jacksonville, FL

I love it when you are in the middle of a pirate battle. And I never get tired of that one drop in the beginning. I even think this attraction's gift shop is cool.

HoT TiP

Some riders can control how high or low the carpet flies. If you want this job, ask to sit in the front row!

The Magic Carpets of Aladdin

If a genie granted you some wishes, what would they be? To be a prince and win the heart of a lovely princess? Well, that was Aladdin's wish, and thanks to his funny friend Genie, his request came true.

You won't find a real genie in this ride, but you will get to take a high-flying trip on a magic carpet—much like Aladdin and Jasmine did in the movie.

The magic touch

Like Dumbo the Flying Elephant in Fantasyland, riders on The Magic Carpets of Aladdin use gears to control their own carpet's flight.

Also like Dumbo, these magic carpets really soar. Beware of the golden camel—he likes to spit at Magic Kingdom guests!

A whole new world

Kids who made a visit to Adventureland before may notice that this land now has a special look. The different shops and decorations make it look a bit like the busy marketplace of Agrabah from *Aladdin*. You might even see the characters from the movie during your visit. So keep a pen handy for autographs when you're in the area.

Swiss Family Treehouse

Before he wrote a book called *The Swiss Family Robinson*, Johann Wyss and his kids imagined what it would be like for their family to be stranded on an island. Together they came up with lots of crazy adventures for the Robinsons. They survive a shipwreck, fight off pirates, and build the most awesome treehouse in the world.

Walt Disney Productions made a movie based on the book in 1960.

The Swiss Family Treehouse in Adventureland looks just like the treehouse in the film. In it, you climb a staircase to many different levels. Each room has lots to see. The tree itself looks very real, but it's not. It has 300,000 plastic leaves, and concrete roots.

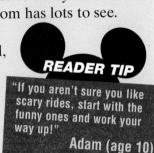

READER TIP

"If you aren't sure you like scary rides, start with the funny ones and work your way up!"

Adam (age 10)
Waynetown, IN

Magic Kingdom

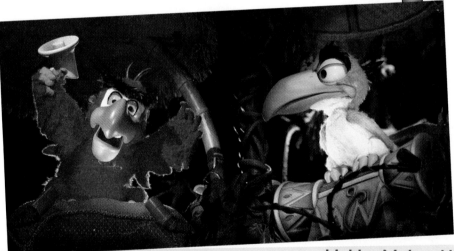

The Enchanted Tiki Room— Under New Management

Hidden Mickey Alert!
Look for a Mickey or two on the bird perches inside the Tiki Room.

Birds rule at this attraction. They also sing and crack lots of jokes. If you've been here before, you may know José, Michael, Fritz, and Pierre. They've been singing old favorites like "The Tiki, Tiki, Tiki Room" for more than 30 years.

Now the Tikis are "Under New Management." They have a new show and new bosses. One is Iago, who's as loud and cranky as he was in *Aladdin*. The other is the very nervous Zazu from *The Lion King*. Thanks to Iago, Zazu has plenty to worry about in this musical show.

23

Frontierland

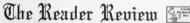

Howdy, pardners! And welcome to the Wild West. Frontierland shows you what America was like when pioneers first settled west of the Mississippi River. It's also where you'll find two of the best rides in the Magic Kingdom. Both of them are special Disney mountains. You can take a watery trip down Splash Mountain and ride a runaway train at Big Thunder Mountain Railroad. These are just a few of the fun things to do here.

HoT TiP

Bring some quarters if you want to play at the Frontierland Shootin' Arcade.

Tom Sawyer Island

There's only one way to get to Tom Sawyer Island—by raft. That's the way Tom himself used to travel. (He is a character created by the author Mark Twain.)

Don't expect to find any rides here. In fact, compared to the rest of the Magic Kingdom, it's a pretty calm place. But if you bring your imagination, you can have exciting adventures of your own.

Bouncy bridges and secret exits

The island has a real windmill to wander through, hills to climb, and two neat bridges. One of them is an old barrel bridge. When one person bounces on it, everyone does.

Across one bridge is a big fort. An Audio-Animatronics blacksmith is working inside it. And there's a secret exit that is really a path through a dark and narrow cave.

In all, there are three caves to explore. They are the best things on the island. Beware: The caves are dark and may be a little scary.

Younger kids love it here

All of Tom Sawyer Island is popular with younger kids. Older kids think the bridges and caves are the best part.

If Aunt Polly's is open, stop by for a snack. It's a nice place to give your feet a rest, too.

HoT TiP

If you sit in the front or on the right side of the log, you get really wet!

Hidden Mickey Alert!

Look in the clouds during the final riverboat scene for a sleeping Mickey. (It comes after the big splash.)

Splash Mountain

READER #1 RIDE PLEASER

After riding Splash Mountain, you'll know how it got its name. It's impossible to stay dry! There are three small dips leading up to a giant, watery drop.

You're all wet

No matter which seat you sit in, there's a good chance you'll get wet. But if you sit in the front, you're sure to get soaked! Don't worry, you'll dry off fast in the Florida sun.

The scenery tells a story

Kids agree that you have to go on it a few times before you can understand the ride's story. (You travel through scenes from Walt Disney's movie *Song of the South*.) Br'er Rabbit is trying to get away

from Br'er Fox and Br'er Bear. When the rabbit goes over the edge toward the end, you go along for the ride. (Try to keep your eyes open during the big drop—it won't be easy.)

You must be at least 40 inches tall to ride.

Hidden Mickey Alert!

This Hidden Mickey is a prickly one—it's part of a cactus at Big Thunder's exit.

READER TIP

"During the parade is a good time to go on the most popular attractions—their lines will be shorter than usual."

Joe (age 13)
Roanoke, VA

ROUGH
Attraction Reaction

Magic Kingdom

Big Thunder Mountain Railroad

DISNEY'S FASTPASS

READER #6 RIDE PLEASER

Hang on to your hat, because this is one of the wildest rides in the wilderness. The speedy trains zip in, out, and over a huge mountain. They pass through scenes with real-looking chickens, goats, donkeys, and more.

The swoops and turns make this a thrilling roller coaster, but it's a lot tamer than Space Mountain. It's a ride you can go on again and again, and see new things each time. Look for funny sights in the town—like the poor guy floating around in a bathtub. Try to ride during the day and again at night.

You must be at least 40 inches tall to ride.

The Reader Review

By: Bryan, age 11
Winchester, VA

The details like the cactus and the animals on the mountain make the ride seem so real. The twists and turns are the best!

Country Bear Jamboree

You've never seen bears quite like these. They sing songs, play instruments, and tell jokes. This is a silly show, so be sure to go in with a silly attitude. Big Al is one of the most popular bears. And he can't even carry a tune!

Everyone gets in on the act

Sometimes the audience sings and claps along with the performers. Even the furry heads on the wall get into the act. (Melvin the moose, Buff the buffalo, and Buck the deer like to *hang* around the theater.)

What do kids think of the bears?

The country music show gets mixed reviews from kids. Some love it. Others aren't so thrilled. But everyone agrees that younger kids like it the most.

The Reader Review

By: Katherine, age 12
Lowell, MA

This is more of a little kids' attraction—but if you go with your little sister, you won't be bored. It's funny. Don't leave this off your list!

Liberty Square

What did America look like in Colonial days? Parts of it looked like Liberty Square! This small area separates Frontierland from Fantasyland. It's a quiet spot with some shops and a couple of popular attractions.

Hidden Mickey Alert!
The gravestones in one of The Haunted Mansion's last rooms bear tiny three-circle Mickeys.

The Haunted Mansion

This haunted house isn't too scary, but there are plenty of ghosts to keep you on your toes. Before you enter, read the funny tombstones in the graveyard outside. (We love the one that says: HERE LIES GOOD OLD FRED. A GREAT BIG ROCK FELL ON HIS HEAD.)

Once inside, you'll be stranded in a room with no windows and no doors. For a while, it seems like there's no way out.

There's a moment before you board your "Doom Buggy" when the room is totally dark. It only lasts a few seconds, but for some, it's much too long.

The car doesn't move very fast, but it's still hard to catch all the details. Watch for the door knockers that knock all by themselves, a ghostly teapot pouring tea, and a ghost napping under the table at a party in the old ballroom.

The Reader Review

By: Staci, age 9
Pleasantville, NY

I was nervous before I went inside the Haunted Mansion, but I didn't need to be. The hitchhiking ghosts and dancing spirits were funny! Everyone will enjoy it.

The Hall of Presidents

The first part of this attraction is a film about our government. Then the screen rises and all the American presidents are on stage together. They are Audio-Animatronics, but they look real. How many presidents can you name in the photo above?

During the show, some of the presidents actually speak. (President George W. Bush recorded his own voice. Abraham Lincoln's voice is performed by an actor.) If you watch closely, you'll notice the presidents move, whisper, and even doze off.

The Reader Review

By: Amy, age 11
Toms River, NJ

It's amazing how real the presidents look. Kids interested in history will really enjoy the show, but others might find it too long and boring.

Liberty Belle Riverboat

The *Liberty Belle* Riverboat docks in Liberty Square. This big steamboat takes guests on slow, relaxing cruises. It can be a nice break on a hot day. The best spots are right up front or in the back, where you can see both sides of the river as you float along.

Mickey's Toontown Fair

Are you looking for that world-famous mouse? You're sure to find him at Mickey's Toontown Fair. He has a job here and, of course, he does it well.

This is the newest land in the Magic Kingdom. It must be a great place because Mickey, Minnie, and their friends all have country homes here. Everywhere you look, you see colorful tents. That's because the county fair is always in town. Guess who's the head judge. (Hint: Think of the mouse who does a good job.)

To get here, follow the path from the Mad Tea Party or from Space Mountain. Or take a ride on the Walt Disney World Railroad.

HoT TiP
Mickey's Toontown Fair is a great place to meet the characters.

Donald's Boat

A popular stop in Toontown is Donald's Boat. It's called the *Miss Daisy*, and it's full of leaks. When you pull the whistle, water shoots out the top. To get to the boat, cross the "duck pond"—another great spot to get wet. Plan to visit Donald's Boat in the early afternoon, when the sun is at its strongest.

READER TIP

"The Barnstormer isn't just for little kids. It's loads of fun for everyone!"

Richard (age 13)
Cooper City, FL

The Barnstormer

The only ride in Toontown Fair is the roller coaster at Goofy's Wiseacre Farm. The ride may look small, but it packs plenty of thrills.

During the trip, a plane takes you on a wild tour of Goofy's farm. It starts out slow, but watch out! You're about to crash into Goofy's barn. The hole in the wall tells you that someone has been there before you. Yes, it's clumsy old Goofy.

Before you ride The Barnstormer, spend some time exploring Goofy's farm. Some of his vegetables are

pretty wacky, just like him. Be sure to look up. Only Goofy would park his airplane in a water tower! You must be at least 35 inches tall to ride.

The Reader Review

By: Daniel, age 11
Plano, TX

This ride is so much fun, it's even fun to wait in the line (which is usually short). I love it when you crash through Goofy's barn and frighten the chickens!

Mickey's Country House

The door is open, so come on in! Mickey's country house tells you a lot about him. His gameroom is full of sports stuff. But the kitchen is a mess. That must be what happens when you let Donald Duck and Goofy decorate!

Where's Mickey? He's hard at work in the Judge's Tent. Walk out the back door of the house and follow the path. You can't miss it! On your way, check out Mickey's garden. Even the vegetables have Mouse ears.

Hidden Mickey Alert!
In Toontown, the Mickeys are practically everywhere! Look for them on plants, benches, lampposts, and windows.

Minnie's Country House

Go ahead, climb on the furniture—Minnie won't mind. There's lots to see and touch in this house. Press the button on the answering machine and listen to Minnie's messages. Open the fridge and feel the cold air. And get set for a trick when you try to take a cookie off her table.

Once you've explored inside, head for Minnie's backyard. She is a very good gardener. On your way there, take a look at the funny flowers in the sunroom. The palm tree has hands, the tiger lilies have tiger faces, and the tulips all have two lips!

Judge's Tent

You found him! Mickey is here all day long, ready to have his picture taken with you. There's always a long wait, but the line is shorter late in the day.

Toontown Hall of Fame

This tent is filled with goodies to buy. But the real reason to come here is to meet Disney characters. They're hanging out in three different rooms. You have to stand in a separate line to enter each room. If you're wondering which characters are available, just read the signs. The Disney princesses have a room all to themselves. It pays to be a princess!

Fantasyland

Fantasyland is home to a lot of magical rides that younger kids just love. Older kids and even grown-ups enjoy them, too. These attractions are very popular, and the waits can be long. But the lines are usually shorter while people are watching the afternoon parade. So it's a good idea to skip the parade one day and spend time in Fantasyland. Plan to catch the parade on another day.

Ariel's Grotto

There is a mysterious blue cave tucked behind Dumbo the Flying Elephant. Inside, there is a special surprise—and her name is Ariel. The star of *The Little Mermaid* is waiting to meet you in her grotto (grotto is another word for cave). Ask her to sign the autograph section that starts on page 144.

Out front, there are some fun fountains to play in, so it's a great place to get wet and cool off when it's hot out. Younger kids especially love splashing around.

The Reader Review

By: Katherine, age 13
Pittsburgh, PA

This is the only place you can meet Ariel in person, so it's a must if you're a *Little Mermaid* fan. But be prepared for a long line!

HoT TiP

Belle from *Beauty and the Beast* sometimes reads stories and signs autographs in Fairytale Garden by Cinderella Castle. Check a park Times Guide to see what time she'll appear during your visit.

Cinderella's Golden Carrousel

Just about all of the attractions at Walt Disney World were dreamed up by Disney Imagineers. But not the carousel. It was discovered in New Jersey, where it was once part of another amusement park. It was built around 1917.

When you climb on a horse for your ride on the carousel, be sure to notice that each one is different. And remember to look up at the ceiling and its hand-painted scenes from *Cinderella*. While you ride, enjoy famous Disney tunes, including "When You Wish Upon a Star" and "Be Our Guest."

READER TIP

"If you want to meet Cinderella, try to have breakfast or lunch at Cinderella's Royal Table in the castle. She'll be there!"
Christine (age 10)
Horsham, PA

ROUGH
Attraction Reaction

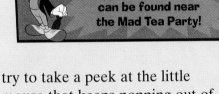

HoT TiP

Sometimes characters from *Alice in Wonderland* can be found near the Mad Tea Party!

Mad Tea Party

The idea for the giant teacups that spin through this ride came from a famous scene in *Alice in Wonderland*. In the movie, the Mad Hatter throws himself a tea party to celebrate his un-birthday. That's any day of the year that isn't his birthday!

On the Mad Tea Party ride, you control how fast your cup spins by turning the big wheel in the center. The more you turn, the more you spin. Or you can just sit back and let the cup spin on its own. It may be hard while you're whirling, but try to take a peek at the little mouse that keeps popping out of the big teapot in the center.

The Reader Review

 A Great Big Beautiful Day!

By: Elizabeth, age 11
Jackson, GA

This ride is fun for the whole family. It's best when everyone helps spin. But if you get dizzy easily, don't turn the wheel, and try not to look outside of your cup as it spins!

The Reader Review

*By: Rachel, age 10
Franklin, TN*

I think this ride is more fun if you go on it with your little brother or sister. I like that you can control how high or low you want to be.

Dumbo the Flying Elephant

Just like the star of the movie *Dumbo*, these elephants know how to fly. They'd love to take you for a short ride (about two minutes) above Fantasyland. A button lets you control the up-and-down movement of the elephant.

Take your kid brother or sister

Many kids agree that this ride is more fun for younger kids, from ages 3 to 8. But they all find something to like, and think it would be fun to go on with a younger brother or sister.

Beware of long lines

Even though Disney added more Dumbos a few years ago, lines for this attraction tend to be long. So if you want to ride, head to Dumbo as soon as you get to the Magic Kingdom. If the line is already too long when you get there, try again toward the end of the day, when the youngest kids may have already gone home.

HOT TIP

If the line here is too long, check out the Magic Carpets of Aladdin in Adventureland. It's a similar ride.

Peter Pan's Flight

Swoop and soar through scenes that tell the story of how Wendy, Michael, and John get sprinkled with pixie dust and fly off to Never Land with Peter Pan and Tinker Bell. Along the way, you meet up with Princess Tiger Lily, the evil Captain Hook, and his sidekick, Mr. Smee.

Near the beginning of the trip, there's a beautiful scene of London at night. Notice that the cars on the streets really move. Later, watch out for the crocodile that wants to eat Captain Hook.

When you first board your pirate ship, it seems like you're riding on a track on the ground. Once you get going, the track is actually above you, so it feels like the ship is really flying.

The Reader Review

By: Kersie, age 12
Vancouver, WA

There are so many interesting things to look at. First you fly high above London. But once you start to see mermaids, you know you're in Never Land!

37

Hidden Mickey Alert!
Many Mickeys can be found in the vines you see in the African scene.

PHOTO BY JILL SAFRO

READER #9 RIDE PLEASER

Magic Kingdom

It's a Small World

People have a lot in common, no matter where they live. That's the point of this attraction. In it, you take a slow boat ride through several large rooms where singing dolls represent different parts of the world. There are Greek dancers, Japanese kite flyers, Scottish bagpipers, and many more. There's also a jungle scene with hippos, giraffes, and monkeys.

All this colorful scenery is set to the song "It's a Small World." Pay attention to the costumes on the dolls and try to guess which country they're from.

The Reader Review

A Great Big Beautiful Day!

By: Joshua, age 13
Plainview, NY

This is my favorite ride. It's fun to try to guess what country the dolls are from. The ride is long and relaxing. It's good for all ages.

38

"Hooray!"

READER TIP

"Get your Fastpass early in the day. They might be all given away by evening!"

Christopher (age 11)
Valley View, OH

DISNEY'S FASTPASS

The Many Adventures of Winnie the Pooh

Winnie the Pooh loves his honey. In fact, he'll do anything to keep the sweet treat safe. On this dizzying trip through the Hundred-Acre Wood, see what Pooh must do to rescue his honey pots and his friends, too.

The blustery day

The wind is howling, the leaves are rustling, and everything in Pooh's world is blowing away. Roo and Piglet are up in the air. Even Owl's house is about to topple over. You better hang on to your honey pot, or you just might be swept away next!

A sticky situation

Finally the wind calms and Pooh can get to sleep. But when he wakes up from his silly dream, it's raining outside. Pooh's honey pots are about to wash away. He can save them, but will he save himself?

The Reader Review
A Great Big Beautiful Day!

By: Kevin, age 13
Danville, IN

This ride was a huge hit with my little brother. My favorite part was the flood scene, when the honey pot you are riding in starts to float around. It's a very sweet ride.

Hidden Mickey Alert!
Mickey is hiding on the mural in Snow White's waiting area. He's by the flowers!

Snow White's Scary Adventures

This attraction takes you through scenes from the movie *Snow White and the Seven Dwarfs*. Some scenes are sweet, while others are scary. If you like Snow White, you're in luck. She is in a lot of scenes (but so is the nasty old witch). Don't expect to see much of the Dwarfs—they don't show up a lot.

There are lots of turns, and the witch seems to be around each one of them. It's very dark during most of the ride, so it can get pretty creepy—especially for younger kids.

Some kids aren't sure who this ride is meant for. It's too scary for many small children and a little simple for older kids. But it's still a classic Disney ride, so try to ride at least once during your visit.

The Reader Review

By: Monet, age 9
Mississauga, Ontario, Canada

They don't call this ride scary for nothing! Even my 13-year-old cousin was scared. It's dark, and that nasty old witch is everywhere! I recommend this ride for people age 8 and up (if they aren't afraid of witches).

Mickey's PhilharMagic

It's magical. It's musical. It's three-dimensional. It's Mickey's PhilharMagic!

Mickey Mouse is the star of this 3-D movie, but it's not a one-mouse show. Mickey is joined by characters such as Donald Duck, Ariel, Aladdin, Jasmine, and Simba. (He starred in the attraction that used to be here: The Legend of the Lion King.)

A one and a two and a three-D

The show takes place in a grand concert hall. Once guests (that's you!) find seats and put on special 3-D glasses, it's showtime.

Sit back, relax, and enjoy as the cast of characters show off their musical talents. (Some are more talented than others.) And be sure to keep your eyes and ears open—a whole lot happens at once.

Eye-popping 3-D effects take place on the oversize screen. Music fills the air. And special surprises happen inside the theater.

What's a PhilharMagic?

In case you were wondering . . . Walt Disney World made up the word PhilharMagic. It's based on the real word *philharmonic*, which describes a bunch of musicians who all play their instruments at the same time.

Magic Kingdom

Tomorrowland

Tomorrowland began as a peek at the future. But as the real world changed, so did this land. Now, it's like a city from a science-fiction story. The palm trees are made of metal. The rides here let you rocket through space or zoom through the Magic Kingdom sky. And a silly alien even pops in for a visit! A good way to see this land is to ride on the Tomorrowland Transit Authority—it's relaxing and it never has a long line.

Hidden Mickey Alert!

This Hidden Mickey is from outer space! When three meteors crash on the ceiling of Space Mountain, they form a giant Mickey head.

Tomorrowland Transit Authority

This slow-moving ride travels by or through most of Tomorrowland's attractions. If you're not sure about going on Space Mountain, the view from here can help you decide. You will also get a peek at Buzz Lightyear's Space Ranger Spin. But pay attention, because you pass by the window pretty quickly.

This ride is a good one to head to when it's really hot outside. The cars move just fast enough to create a nice breeze. It's also interesting to know that the ride doesn't give off any pollution.

The Reader Review

By: Ashley, age 14
Lockport, NY

This ride isn't always given the attention it deserves. It's a fun way to travel above Tomorrowland. I like to go on it during the light parade at night. The view is great.

Space Mountain

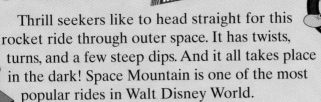

Thrill seekers like to head straight for this rocket ride through outer space. It has twists, turns, and a few steep dips. And it all takes place in the dark! Space Mountain is one of the most popular rides in Walt Disney World.

Who turned out the lights?!

It's so dark inside Space Mountain that you barely see where you are going—especially if you sit in the front of the rocket. That's what makes the ride so thrilling. Every curve comes as a surprise!

Sometimes you'll hear the sounds of other rockets zooming by, and it seems like you might crash into them. But don't worry: The coaster is perfectly safe. Those noises are just meant to add to the excitement.

Is it too scary?

Everyone agrees: Space Mountain is scary! But some kids say it's a "good scary." Anything that was "bad scary" happened only in their imagination. In fact, the rockets only travel about 28 miles per hour. That makes it one of the slower roller coasters in Walt Disney World. But you'd never guess it! You must be at least 44 inches tall to ride.

Magic Kingdom

The Reader Review

By: Alexandra, age 13
Lindenhurst, NY

This is one of the coolest rides in Disney! The beginning is awesome. I love the flashing lights in the tunnel. After that, it's all downhill (literally!). It's dark, so you never know where you are going to turn next.

Walt Disney's Carousel of Progress

A lot has changed since the year 1900. There was no electricity, water came from a well, and nobody had a TV. Life was rough! This attraction shows how American family life has changed since then.

The show is really four short plays. And the performers are all Audio-Animatronics actors. After each scene, the theater moves to the right. That's when you'll hear the song "There's a Great, Big, Beautiful Tomorrow." Feel free to sing along!

Some kids may find the show a bit on the slow side, but others think it's quite special. Why? It was introduced to the world by Walt Disney himself. The special event didn't happen at Disney World (it wasn't open yet), but at the World's Fair in New York City in 1964. Of course, the attraction has been updated (there has been a lot of progress since then), but the show is still an amusing look at American life. And the Carousel of Progress has made history, too—it's had more performances than any other show in the history of American theater.

The Reader Review

By: Faith, age 10
Torrington, CT

This is one of my family's favorite attractions. I recommend it for when you need to take a break from all the excitement and relax.

Stitch's Great Escape!

There is a cuddly alien prisoner who needs guarding. Do you think you can keep him from escaping? Even if the alien is that mischievous rascal named Stitch? This silly attraction asks Magic Kingdom guests to keep an eye on the little guy and keep him out of trouble. **Good luck!**

Of course, Stitch rarely does what he's told. When he does escape, his silly antics keep everyone laughing. And the special effects make it seem like the little alien is running around the room. Don't be surprised if he sneaks up beside you, whispers in your ear, and musses your hair. (He never had very good manners!) **Stitch can escape, but you can't!**

Don't be alarmed when a harness comes down as the show starts. It's just there to make the effects more special. It'll lift up automatically at the end of the adventure. (Be sure to sit up straight when it first comes down and let it tap your shoulders.) Everyone must be at least 40 inches tall to enter Stitch's Great Escape.

Hidden Mickey Alert!

Watch the planets carefully as they whiz by during the short movie. One of them is extra special—it has a Mickey on it!

Buzz Lightyear's Space Ranger Spin

In this attraction, everyone is a toy—including you. In fact, you are so small, you fit inside a video game shooting gallery.

To infinity and beyond!

The ride is under the command of Buzz Lightyear. You've just become a Junior Space Ranger, so you're under his command, too. Together, you battle the evil Emperor Zurg.

Zap that Zurg

Zurg and his robots are stealing batteries from other toys. They plan to use the batteries to power their ultimate weapon of destruction. Your job is to fight back. Use the laser cannons in your spaceship to aim at the targets (they look like Zs) and zap Zurg's power. Every time you hit a target, you earn more points. There is a scoreboard by your cannon that keeps track of your points.

At the end of the ride, you'll pass a chart. It shows everyone's ranger rank based on their score. Check to see where your score falls. Most kids improve with practice.

The Reader Review

By: Liza, age 15
Atlanta, GA

The fact that this ride is interactive makes it really cool. I was pretty bad, but I definitely had a blast. It's dark, but not too scary for younger kids. I think almost everyone will like this ride. Even my parents had fun!

Monsters, Inc.—The Laugh Floor

Stitch has some new neighbors here in Tomorrowland—Mike, Roz, and other kooky characters from the hit movie *Monsters, Inc.* They are all part of a silly attraction that lets you interact with your animated friends. That's right, the audience members not only watch the show—they're a part of it! Don't worry. They don't want to make kids scream (the way they did in the movie). This time, they want to make kids laugh. So be prepared for lots of wackiness and a few very bad jokes!

Tomorrowland Indy Speedway

You don't need a license to drive your own car around this racetrack (as long as you're at least 52 inches tall). Cars travel along a track, but it's not as easy to drive as it looks. Even experts bounce around a lot. The cars are real and are powered by gasoline.

The Reader Review

By: Hilary, age 12
Amesburg, MA

This is a fun way to be able to drive. It's perfect for kids ages 7 to 12. Younger kids may need help pushing the pedals, and older kids might not find it as exciting.

READER TIP

"If you're afraid of heights, skip Astro Orbiter!"

Derek (age 13)
Spokane, WA

Astro Orbiter

In the middle of Tomorrowland, there is a giant, glowing tower. It is called Rockettower. The Astro Orbiter ride is all the way at the top. In it, you soar past colorful planets high above Tomorrowland.

Like on Dumbo the Flying Elephant, you control how high or low your rocket flies. You can ride by yourself or with a friend. (Each rocket fits two people.) But if you want to be the one to control how high you go, be sure to sit in the front.

The Reader Review

By: Matthew, age 13
Lakeland, FL

I love going on this ride! Some kids may be scared, but older kids will probably like it best because it goes up very high and tilts when you reach the top.

Entertainment

The Magic Kingdom is a very entertaining place. It seems like there is always a show starting or a parade going by. Read on to learn about some of the special events that take place in the park. For more information, check a park Times Guide. You can get one at the entrance to any Disney theme park, or in the park's shops and restaurants.

fight off a nightmare or two (thanks to that nasty Maleficent!). The show happens every day.

DISNEY DREAMS COME TRUE PARADE

Your favorite Disney characters star in this afternoon parade. You might even get to dance with some characters as they pass by. Be sure to line up early to get a good spot on the curb.

SPECTROMAGIC

This nighttime parade makes its way down Main Street, U.S.A., during busy seasons. Special lighting effects and lots of characters make for a great show. This parade does not run every day. Check a park Times Guide for the schedule.

WISHES

Look—up in the sky! It's not a bird or a plane . . . it's an amazing fireworks show! For the best view of the show, stand right in the middle of Main Street, facing the castle.

DREAM ALONG WITH MICKEY

Do you believe in dreams? You will after you watch this toe-tapping musical show in front of Cinderella Castle. In it, Mickey Mouse and his friends celebrate happy dreams and

Where to find
CHARACTERS
at the MAGIC KINGDOM

Characters greet guests all over the park. A great place to find them is **Mickey's Toontown Fair**. You can meet Mickey in the **Judge's Tent**, and the rest of the gang—including Disney princesses—are in the **Toontown Hall of Fame**.

Characters from Disney movies like *Peter Pan* sometimes hang out in **Adventureland**. Alice in Wonderland and her friends prefer **Fantasyland**, while Br'er Rabbit and Br'er Bear enjoy spending time near **Splash Mountain**.

If you want to meet the Little Mermaid, go to **Ariel's Grotto** in Fantasyland (the line may be long, but her fans think it's worth the wait!).

When you're in **Tomorrowland**, keep an eye out for Buzz Lightyear and Stitch.

Attraction Ratings

COOL
(Check It Out)

- Cinderella's Golden Carrousel
- Snow White's Scary Adventures
- The Hall of Presidents
- Tomorrowland Transit Authority
- Liberty Belle Riverboat
- Swiss Family Treehouse
- The Enchanted Tiki Room—Under New Management
- Monsters, Inc.—The Laugh Floor
- Walt Disney's Carousel of Progress

REALLY COOL
(Don't Miss)

- The Barnstormer
- Astro Orbiter
- Tomorrowland Indy Speedway
- Mad Tea Party
- Country Bear Jamboree
- Jungle Cruise
- Walt Disney World Railroad
- Dumbo the Flying Elephant
- The Magic Carpets of Aladdin
- It's a Small World
- Stitch's Great Escape!
- Tom Sawyer Island

THE COOLEST
(See at Least Twice)

- Space Mountain
- Splash Mountain
- Big Thunder Mountain Railroad
- The Haunted Mansion
- Peter Pan's Flight
- Buzz Lightyear's Space Ranger Spin
- Pirates of the Caribbean
- Mickey's PhilharMagic
- The Many Adventures of Winnie the Pooh

What do YOU think?

The kids who helped with this book rated all the attractions at Walt Disney World. But your opinion counts, too! Make your own "Attraction Ratings" list for each park and send it to us. We'll use it when we create next year's book. (Our address is on page 7.)

Magic Kingdom

TIPS

Head to this park first, since it has the most rides for kids.

Arrive a half hour before the opening time. Walk down Main Street to get a head start before the rest of the park opens.

Check the Tip Board on Main Street, U.S.A. It lists the wait times for the most popular Magic Kingdom attractions.

Rest your feet and watch a movie starring Mickey in the Exposition Hall on Main Street. Afterward, you can pose for pictures in front of famous Disney backgrounds. Sometimes characters hang out there, too!

Need to cool off on a hot day? You can get soaked at Ariel's Grotto in Fantasyland, Donald's Boat in Mickey's Toontown Fair, or Cool Ship in Tomorrowland.

If the park is open late, it's fun to go on your favorite attractions again after dark.

There are "chicken exits" in the lines for all scary rides, just in case you change your mind about riding at the last minute.

Never eat just before riding The Barnstormer, Astro Orbiter, Space Mountain, Big Thunder Mountain Railroad, or the Mad Tea Party.

If you've never been on a roller coaster, ride The Barnstormer first. If you like it, try Big Thunder Mountain Railroad next. Save Space Mountain for last—it's the scariest.

If there are two lines at an attraction, the one on the left is usually shorter.

Epcot

Epcot is a great place to make discoveries about the world. At this theme park, things that used to seem ordinary suddenly become fun. All of the attractions at Epcot are in buildings called pavilions. The pavilions are in two sections of the park. One section is Future World, and the other is World Showcase. Future World celebrates inventions and ideas. It shows how they affect everything, from the land, sea, sky, and outer space to your mind and body.

World Showcase lets you travel around the world without leaving the park! There are many different countries to visit here. Each country has copies of its famous buildings, restaurants, and other landmarks. Together, they make you feel as if you're visiting the real place.

FUTURE WORLD

Epcot

JAPAN

MOROCCO

FRANCE

INTERNATIONAL GATEWAY

AMERICAN ADVENTURE

UNITED KINGDOM

ITALY

CANADA

IMAGINATION!

GERMANY

WORLD SHOWCASE LAGOON

THE LAND

CHINA

THE SEAS

NORWAY

SHOWCASE PLAZA

INNOVENTIONS WEST

MEXICO

TEST TRACK

INNOVENTIONS EAST

MISSION: SPACE

WONDERS OF LIFE

UNIVERSE OF ENERGY

SPACESHIP EARTH

To Buses

Entrance Plaza

N

Future World

When you enter Epcot by monorail, you are in the area called Future World. Many of the attractions here are educational—but that doesn't mean you won't have fun. Take it from other kids: There's a lot to discover.

SPACESHIP EARTH

You can't miss the giant silver ball that is the symbol of Epcot. It's gigantic! The Spaceship Earth ride is inside this big, round building. (It's called a geosphere.) The slow-moving ride explores the different ways people have communicated with each other throughout history. You'll see the different ways people have sent messages over the years.

A highlight of the trip is when the time machine vehicle reaches the top of the building. Look up and you'll think you are staring into a night sky. The stars are beautiful.

The Reader Review

By: Amy, age 12
Clinton, NJ

Some people think this ride is not worth a long wait, but it's one of my family's favorites. It may be a calm ride, but I think it's very interesting. It's a classic!

Epcot

MISSION: SPACE

ROUGH — Attraction Reaction

LOUD — Attraction Reaction

DARK — Attraction Reaction

FASTPASS

Three ... two ... one ... blast-off! This ride lets you know what it's like to be an astronaut on a trip to outer space. In this case, you are on a mission to Mars.

Each spacecraft holds four guests. Once aboard, it's time for takeoff. You'll really feel the tug of gravity during the launch—just like on a NASA space shuttle. This part lasts nearly a minute, so be ready.

What's your job?

Once you're on your way, things calm down a bit. That may be when you realize you have a job to do. Are you the commander, engineer, pilot, or navigator? That depends on where you sit. It doesn't matter—all the jobs are fun to do. Just before you land, you will get a strange sensation. It's not weightlessness, but it is definitely out of this world. It's a lot like the feeling astronauts get in outer space.

Mission accomplished

You must be at least 44 inches tall to take either training mission into space. If bouncing or spinning makes you sick, skip the intense trip—a lot of people get woozy on it. Some even feel sick afterward. If you're not tall enough or would like a calmer ride, you can take a tamer trip to Mars at this attraction. Ask for the "less intense" ride at the entrance. Kids love it.

Chill out!

Do you need a place to escape from the heat? Head to Club Cool in Innoventions Plaza. Inside you can sample sodas from around the world. The best part? The samples are free! Some of the sodas are yummy, but most kids think one is just plain yucky. Are you brave enough to taste them all?

HoT TiP

Finding your way around this pavilion is a snap with an Innoventions map. Pick one up at the entrance.

READER TIP

"Watch the sidewalk outside Innoventions at night. It sparkles!"

David (age 7)
Reading, PA

INNOVENTIONS

Here's your chance to try out some interesting new inventions. You can also talk on a giant phone, send a video postcard to a friend by e-mail, or experience high-tech virtual reality games.

On the road again

At Innoventions, you travel down "The Road to Tomorrow." Along the way, stop at each of the interesting exhibits. Some of them teach you about new technologies, while others show you recent inventions for the home or tell you about discoveries in science.

Street smarts

Tom Morrow is your tour guide at Innoventions. He's an Audio-Animatronics robot who will keep you from getting lost during your trip. There are road signs and street maps, too. Still can't find what you are looking for? Simply ask a cast member to lead you on your way.

The Seas with Nemo & Friends

It's easy to find Nemo these days—he's at The Seas pavilion at Epcot! He and his friends can't wait for you to visit. There are more than 2,000 real sea creatures living here. There's also a cool ride, a play area, and cool sea-related exhibits to explore.

The Seas with Nemo & Friends

Jump inside a clam-mobile and let the adventure begin! It's a class trip run by Nemo's teacher, Mr. Ray. It seems little Nemo has wandered off again. Your job is to help find him. Expect to meet up with Dory, Bruce, Chum, Squirt, and others along the way. And don't worry—Nemo won't stay lost for long.

Hands-on Fun

After a quick look at the aquarium, you enter an area called Sea Base. This is your chance to take a closer look at the creatures and to try out the hands-on exhibits. Be sure to visit the Nemo and Friends room, where you can find a real-life version of the little guy. Younger kids get a kick out of Bruce's Sharkhouse. (It's a play area where you can learn about sharks.)

Talk to the Turtle

Everyone seems to love Turtle Talk with Crush. It's a show that lets you talk to the cartoon critter. The best part? He talks back. It is totally awesome, dude!

THE LAND

The building called The Land looks like a big greenhouse. Some of its attractions focus on food and where it comes from. There's a boat ride, and a movie about the environment. It stars Simba, Timon, and Pumbaa from *The Lion King*. Soarin' is another ride here. It lets guests fly high in the sky.

Hidden Mickey Alert!

Study the paintings while you wait in line for Living with the Land. One has bubbles on it that connect to form a Mickey head.

Living with the Land

Disney's FASTPASS

What's the most popular fruit on our planet? The banana! People eat more bananas than any other fruity snack. You'll learn lots more food facts on this boat trip. The boat travels through rooms that look like a rain forest, desert, and prairie. Then it heads to a modern greenhouse area.

A recording explains all the things your boat floats past. If you're lucky, you'll see some giant vegetables growing here. The greenhouse has produced some of the biggest lemons and eggplants in the world!

In all, The Land grows more than 30 tons of fruit and veggies each year. A lot of it is served to guests in Epcot restaurants, like the Garden Grill and Coral Reef.

The Reader Review

By: Sean, age 8
Schenectady, NY

I thought this ride was fun, and it taught me a lot about nature. I especially liked visiting the greenhouse. It was neat to see all sorts of plants from all around the world growing under one roof.

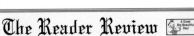

The Reader Review

By: Gianna, age 10
Pembroke Pines, FL

I love this ride because you fly over beautiful lands. When you fly over orange trees, you can smell the oranges! The flying part might be scary for younger kids.

Soarin'

Have you ever wondered what it's like to be a bird? To swoop and soar high above the ground and way up into the clouds? This new attraction lets you experience that first-hand.

Fasten your safety belt

Before the fun starts, you'll grab a seat in one of the many hang gliders. Put your valuables in the basket, fasten your seat belt, sit back, and get ready.

Up, up, and away!

As your glider lifts off the ground, a gigantic movie screen lights up in front of you. On it, you'll see many different scenes from the state of California. During the journey, flyers glide past Yosemite Valley, the Golden Gate Bridge, and the desert in Death Valley. Many scenes were filmed using special cameras on airplanes and helicopters. Your glider moves the same way those aircraft did—so it feels like you're really flying.

How real does it feel? Some people lift their feet when they fly over the forest—because it seems like their toes will hit the treetops! At one point, it even smells real (the orange grove smells orangy!).

The whole trip takes about four minutes. You must be at least 40 inches tall to ride. If you get motion sickness or are afraid of heights, you should skip this one.

Hidden Mickey Alert!
Look up in the cloud under the blue balloon at The Land pavilion's center.

The Circle of Life

Simba, Timon, and Pumbaa are together again. This time they're in a movie about the importance of protecting the Earth's environment. The film is a mix of animation and live action. It shows some of the problems we face—and how we can fix them.

Timber!

The movie's opening scene shows animals just like those in *The Lion King* (but these animals are real). Next, you see Simba near a watering hole. All of a sudden he hears "timber!" and is drenched by the splash of a tree falling into water. Timon and Pumbaa are clearing the grassland to build a resort (the Hakuna Matata Lakeside Village).

Simba tells a story

Simba remembers what his father taught him about the importance of caring for the land. He tells Timon and Pumbaa a story about how humans sometimes forget that everything is connected in the great Circle of Life.

The Reader Review

*By: Rachel, age 12
Fort Worth, TX*

What I like about this attraction is that you see pictures of the land before and after humans made a mess of it. It also shows ways we can improve the cleanliness of our world. I recommend it for kids ages 8 and up.

IMAGINATION!

This pavilion is like a workout for your imagination—the attractions really make you think! There is an interesting and fun ride that tests your creativity, a hands-on activity center, and a wacky 3-D movie called *Honey, I Shrunk the Audience*. Outside, the jumping waters of the Leap Frog Fountains are sure to keep you guessing. There are a lot of other ways to have fun here, too. Just use your imagination!

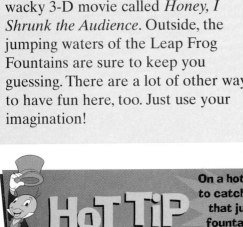

HoT TiP

On a hot day, cool off by trying to catch the streams of water that jump from fountain to fountain at the entertaining Leap Frog Fountains.

ImageWorks

Once you get inside ImageWorks, it may be hard to leave. Kids love it because it's full of hands-on (and feet-on) activities. And now it's even better, because there are lots of new things to see and do.

Most kids agree that one of their favorite stops is Stepping Tones, where you can step on colored lights to trigger different sounds and reactions. Another popular activity is the Electronic Philharmonic. There you can conduct an orchestra just by raising and lowering your hands. And there's so much more, so plan to spend about an hour here.

The Reader Review

A Great Big Beautiful Day!

By: Leah, age 10
Pittsburgh, PA

ImageWorks is really cool! There's a machine that takes your picture and turns it into a flower, animal, or cartoon, and then you can e-mail the photo to a friend!

Journey Into Imagination with Figment

Think how different the world would be without any imagination in it. There would be no stories to tell, no pictures to draw, and no inventions to make things easier. One thing is for sure—Walt Disney World certainly wouldn't exist! Imagination is so important to the folks at Disney that they created a special place in Future World to learn all about it. It's called the Imagination Institute. Here you can go on a trip as far as your mind will take you.

Testing, testing, 1-2-3

The Imagination Institute is having an open house. That means everyone is invited to learn about all of its secret projects. And who better to take you on a tour of this special place than Figment himself? (Figment is a little purple dragon. He was the host of this attraction a few years back. That's him in the photo on the right.)

How do they do that?

There are some special effects during the ride that make the tour even more interesting. You'll experience them in areas known as the Sight Lab, the Sound Lab, and the Smell Lab.

HoT TiP Are you a Figment fan? He went away for a while—but he's back! Look for him at the Journey Into Imagination attraction.

Honey, I Shrunk the Audience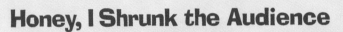

Remember the kids from *Honey, I Shrunk the Kids*? This 3-D movie gives you an idea of how they felt. That's because this time you're the one who gets shrunk, along with the rest of the audience. Even the theater seems to shrink.

Some special effects add to the excitement. You get spooked by hundreds of 3-D mice, a lion, and a very big and scary snake. Then one of the kids from the movie picks up the theater and carries it

around. Somehow you're brought back to real size, but only after some unusual adventures.

The Reader Review

By: Adam, age 11
Frankfort, IL

I don't think this is a good show for young kids. They could get scared by all the mice and the snake (it looks like it's going to bite your head!). But for older kids the show is funny and exciting.

Hidden Mickey Alert!

This Hidden Mickey is a sweet one! In Area 2B, look for a candy dispenser that's in the shape of that famous mouse.

Epcot

TEST TRACK

READER #8 RIDE PLEASER

What is it like to be a crash-test dummy? Find out in this thrilling ride—and learn what new cars go through to be safe for riders.

Where are the brakes?

Test Track is one of Walt Disney World's fastest rides, and Epcot's original thrill ride. The sporty test cars travel on a track that's almost a mile long. Your car has no steering wheel or brake pedals for you to control, but its sound and video equipment lets you know what's being tested. You zip around curves, zoom down a street, and bounce on bumpy roads. At one point, you nearly crash into a truck!

A crash course in car safety

Kids think this ride is a fun way to learn more about cars. Parts of it are loud, so don't be startled if you hear a crash! And don't worry—the ride is safer than it looks. Disney workers tested the cars first. After all, that's what test-driving is all about.

You must be at least 40 inches tall to try it.

After the ride, check out the post-show area. Here you can take a virtual journey at an interesting exhibit called Dreamchasers.

The Reader Review

By: Amanda, age 13
St. Michael, MN

At first, I was afraid to go on this ride, but after I did, it became one of my favorites. I like the way it twists and turns as you go through a test course. It's a thrill ride, but you still learn some things.

WONDERS OF LIFE

You know what you look like on the outside. Now find out what you look like on the inside. This pavilion is all about the human body. This building is only open during Epcot's busiest times. That's usually in summer and during holidays. It might not be open during your visit to the park.

Epcot

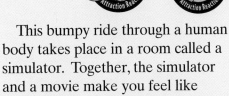
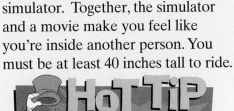

Body Wars

Every time you get a cut, it's white blood cells to the rescue. They destroy infections and help you heal. In this attraction, white blood cells mistake a scientist for an infection. She was shrunk for a special mission inside a body—to remove a nasty splinter. Now the white blood cells are after her! Your mission is to rescue the scientist before it's too late.

This bumpy ride through a human body takes place in a room called a simulator. Together, the simulator and a movie make you feel like you're inside another person. You must be at least 40 inches tall to ride.

HoT TiP
If the sight of blood makes you woozy, don't ride Body Wars.

Hidden Mickey Alert!

This one is a no-brainer! He's easy to spot near Walt Disney on the "Hall of Brains" poster.

Cranium Command

Imagine that you're a pilot. But instead of flying an airplane, you pilot the brain of a 12-year-old boy. That's what happens to Buzzy during this attraction, and you get to go along for the ride.

Buzzy and the brain

During the pre-show, you stand and watch a funny cartoon that explains how Buzzy gets his job. Then you go into a theater—and inside the brain with Buzzy. You watch as he tries to get all the different parts of the brain to work together.

Kids identify with Bobby

The brain in Cranium Command belongs to a boy named Bobby. (The cranium is the part of your skull where your brain is.) It's Buzzy's job to pilot Bobby through a day at school. And what a day it is!

The Reader Review

By: Emily, age 9
Richmond, United Kingdom

Cranium Command is wonderful. I loved every second of it! It was so cool listening to what each part of Bobby's brain had to say. I wish it were even longer!

PHOTO BY JILL SAFRO

Fitness Fairgrounds

The lobby of the Wonders of Life pavilion is filled with hands-on (and feet-on!) activities. You could plan to spend up to a half hour here.

In the Sensory Funhouse, kids enjoy trying to guess what certain objects are without being able to see them. Fitness Fairgrounds is a great place to burn off extra energy and have fun. (The Wonders of Life pavilion may not be open during your visit to Epcot.) You may do a little shopping and munch on a healthy snack here, too.

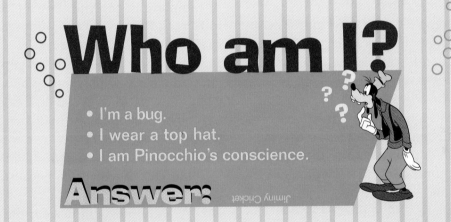

Who am I?

- I'm a bug.
- I wear a top hat.
- I am Pinocchio's conscience.

Answer: Jiminy Cricket

Epcot

The Making of Me

Where do babies come from? That question and many more are answered in the film *The Making of Me*. The movie is shown in a theater in the middle of the Wonders of Life pavilion. It lasts 14 minutes. It's a good show to watch with your parents.

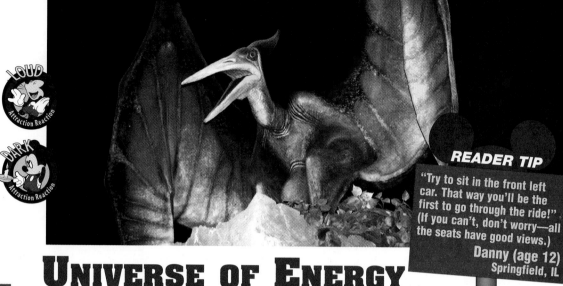

READER TIP

"Try to sit in the front left car. That way you'll be the first to go through the ride!" (If you can't, don't worry—all the seats have good views.)

Danny (age 12)
Springfield, IL

Epcot

UNIVERSE OF ENERGY

Discover where energy comes from on this trip through prehistoric times, complete with dinosaurs. The ride is called Ellen's Energy Adventure. It's inside the Universe of Energy pavilion.

Ellen's energy nightmare

The attraction starts with a movie about a woman named Ellen. She is asleep and having a weird dream. She's a contestant on a TV game show—and all of the questions are about energy. Ellen doesn't know much about energy, so she really stinks at the game.

Then Bill Nye, the Science Guy, decides to teach her all about energy. To do it, he takes her (and you) on a trip back in time.

Visit the dinosaurs

First you go into a theater to see another movie. Then the ride part begins. Bill Nye takes you and Ellen to a prehistoric world. You travel through fog and past several different types of dinosaurs. Some of them are huge. And they all look real. Be careful or one might sneeze on you!

At the end of the ride, Ellen gets another chance to play on the TV game show. How does she do this time? That's something you'll have to see for yourself!

Three cheers for energy!

Some kids like this ride because it's a fun way to learn about energy. But others enjoy it for the dinosaurs. Everyone agrees on one thing: Ellen's Energy Adventure is one of Epcot's best rides.

The Reader Review A Great Big Beautiful Day!

By: Nicholas, age 10
Vancouver, WA

This show is funny and teaches you a lot about where energy comes from. My favorite part is when the theater seats turn into ride cars and start to move!

World Showcase

Anyone can be a world traveler at World Showcase. You can learn about other countries, experience different cultures, and meet people from all over the world. Most of the people who work in each pavilion really come from the country they represent. And they're all happy to talk to you.

The pavilions were built around a lake called World Showcase Lagoon. If you make the trip all the way around the lake, you will walk more than one mile!

Hidden Mickey Alert!

The iron grates that the trees in World Showcase grow out of could probably tell a mouse tale or two! They're covered with Hidden Mickeys!

READER TIP

"If you want to learn more about some of the pavilions in Epcot, stop at Guest Relations. They have lots of interesting fact sheets."

Benjamin (age 11)
Geneseo, NY

CANADA

If you look at a map of North America, Canada is at the top, just above the United States. It's a beautiful country. The Canada pavilion at Epcot is very pretty, too. There's a rocky mountain, a stream, gardens, and a totem pole.

The highlight is a movie called *O Canada!* The scenes completely surround you. Since you stand during the movie, it's easy to turn around and see everything. Most kids enjoy the movie, but wish the theater had seats!

The Reader Review

By: Shelby, age 14
Calgary, Alberta, Canada

This pavilion shows what Canadians are proud of. I should know—I'm from Canada! I wish the film included even more, but it's a great introduction to my country.

UNITED KINGDOM

From London to the English countryside, this pavilion gives a varied view of the United Kingdom. Some details to look for include the smoke stains painted on the chimneys to make them appear old, and the grassy roofs that are really made of plastic broom bristles.

The Reader Review

By: Cody, age 9
Staten Island, NY

Take a picture by the red telephone booths like the ones in England. Also, see if the band is playing in the garden. Older kids and adults will like to hear it play.

International Mouse

Mickey Mouse is famous all over the world. But not everyone knows the movie-star mouse by that name. In Italy he's called Topolino. In Greece he's known as Miky Maoye. Norwegians call him Mikke Mus. In Sweden he goes by Musse Pigg. And in China he's Mi Lao Shu. That's a lot of names for one mouse to remember!

FRANCE

The Eiffel Tower is probably the best-known landmark at the France pavilion. (The real one is in Paris, France.) The buildings here look just like those in a real French town. Many of the workers here come from France. They speak English with a French accent. Surprise them by saying *bonjour* (pronounced: *bohn-zhoor*). It means "good day" in French.

The main attraction—besides the treats at the bakery—is *Impressions de France* (Impressions of France).

It's a movie that takes you from one end of France to the other. It's shown on a big screen, and you get to sit down and take in the sights.

The Reader Review

By: Ryan, age 12
Pepper Pike, OH

I have been to the real France and Epcot's France is just as cool. The food is delicious, especially at the bakery. I think everyone will enjoy the entertainment, shops, and food.

Topiary Trees

There's something unusual about some of the trees growing at Walt Disney World—they're shaped like animals! Some even look like Disney characters. These special plants are called **topiaries** (pronounced:

TOE-pea-air-ees). They're carefully groomed each day by gardeners to keep their exact form. You may spot an Alice topiary by the Mad Tea Party in the Magic Kingdom and a Mary Poppins tree in Epcot's United Kingdom. Disney World has more than 200 topiaries in all. How many can you find?

MOROCCO

The country of Morocco is famous for its mosaics—artwork and patterns that are made up of many tiles. That's why there is beautiful tile work on the walls of this pavilion. Moroccan artists made sure the mosaics here were done right.

The buildings are copies of monuments in Moroccan cities, including Fez and Marrakesh. There are many shops selling items you could find in Morocco. You can buy baskets, brass, jewelry, or sandals, a fez (a type of hat), and other Moroccan clothing.

A belly dancer entertains guests at Marrakesh restaurant. And a band called Mo'Rockin performs in the courtyard.

Salam alekoum (pronounced: *sah-LAHM wah-LAY-koom*) means "hello" in Morocco. (It's Arabic.)

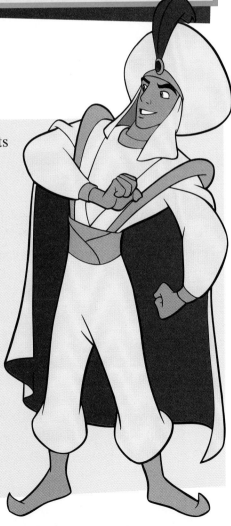

READER TIP

"Try to eat meals early or late in the day to avoid long lines!"

John (age
Washington Township,

JAPAN

The giant temple out front, called a pagoda, makes the Japanese pavilion easy to spot. It's modeled after a famous pagoda in the city of Nara, Japan.

Be sure to notice all of the evergreen trees. In Japan, they are symbols of eternal life. Some of the trees found in a traditional Japanese garden will not survive in Florida. Similar trees were used instead.

Japanese drummers often perform outside the pavilion. The huge department store has lots of souvenirs from Japan.

Want to say "good morning" in Japanese? Just say *ohayo gozaimasu* (pronounced: *oh-hi-yoh goh-zy-ee-mahs*).

Just for Kids!

Epcot has something special for younger kids: Kidcot Fun Stops. There's one in each country of World Showcase, plus Test Track, The Land, and The Seas with Nemo & Friends. At each of these spots, you can color, make crafts, and learn how kids have fun all over the world.

THE AMERICAN ADVENTURE

The United States of America is the star of this pavilion. That's why it's called the American Adventure.

The American Adventure show takes place inside a building that looks a bit like Independence Hall (the real Independence Hall is in Philadelphia, Pennsylvania). The show celebrates the American spirit throughout our history.

Benjamin Franklin and Mark Twain host the show. They look so real, you may forget that they are mechanical. Ben Franklin even walks up stairs!

The American Adventure show honors many heroes from history: the Pilgrims, Alexander Graham Bell, Jackie Robinson, Susan B. Anthony, Walt Disney, and others. It's a great way to learn about American history.

The Reader Review

By: Joshua, age 12
Cheektowaga, NY

The American Adventure is educational yet entertaining. It is impossible to leave without a smile on your face and a true feeling of pride for being an American.

Hidden Mickey Alert!

Let your eyes follow the fireworks that burst from behind the Statue of Liberty. One of them leaves a Mickey-shaped puff of smoke (in the American Adventure).

ITALY

Venice is an Italian city known for waterways called canals. There are no canals at Epcot's Italy, but the pavilion does look a lot like the real thing. The tower is a smaller version of the Campanile, a famous building in Venice. Notice the gondolas (pronounced: *GAHN-doe-lahs*) tied to the dock in the lagoon. They are a type of boat used for traveling in the canals of Venice.

Say *buon giorno* (pronounced: *boo-on JOR-no*). It means "good day" in Italian.

GERMANY

Hidden Mickey Alert!
You'll find a Mickey in the grass in Germany's miniature village.

There isn't a village in Germany quite like the one at Epcot. It's a combination of cities and small towns from all around the country. Try to stop by the pavilion on the hour so you can see the special cuckoo clock near the toy shop and hear it chime.

In German, "good day" is *guten tag* (say: *GOOT-en tahkh*).

The Reader Review

By: Micheline, age 9
Coral Springs, FL

Germany is one of my favorite pavilions. I love the cuckoo clocks, teddy bears, and sausages! A great time to visit Germany is in October for Oktoberfest. There are special games, food, singing, and dancing!

Who am I?

- I wear glasses.
- I'm not very tall.
- I have six roommates.

Answer: Doc

CHINA

Disney's version of the Temple of Heaven is at the center of this pavilion. It's a landmark in the Chinese city of Beijing. Inside, there is a Circle-Vision 360 movie called *Reflections of China*. (There are no seats in the theater.)

Before going in to see the movie, take a look at the waiting area. It's decorated in red and gold. These colors mean good luck in China.

The film takes guests on a tour of the country. It's worth seeing, but it is more popular with adults than kids. Most kids would rather spend their time checking out the fish in the pond or watching the acrobats perform in the courtyard.

To say "hello" in Chinese, say *ni hao* (pronounced: *nee HOW*).

The Reader Review

By: Beckie, age 9
St. Gettysburg, PA

I really like China. It's got massive gift shops, a pond with fish, and lots of food, plus a movie!. I could spend a year—and a lot of money here!

HoT TiP

Go to Maelstrom late in the day, when the line is shorter.

Hidden Mickey Alert!
Look in the mural above the line for a Viking wearing Mickey Mouse ears.

READER TIP

"Sit in the back of the boat on Maelstrom for the best view."

Sam (age 15)
San Diego, CA

Epcot

NORWAY

You will discover the history and culture of Norway at this pavilion. (Don't worry about the angry troll. He's harmless.)

The main building is a castle. It was based on an ancient fortress in the capital city of Oslo. Inside, there is a ride called Maelstrom. It's about Norway's history.

The ride begins in a Viking village. (Vikings were explorers who lived about 1,000 years ago. Many came from Norway.) Next you travel to a forest, where a three-headed troll curses your

boat and makes it go backward! After the boat trip, there is a short movie about Norway.

Saying "hello" is easy here. It's *god dag* (say: *goo DAHG*).

The Reader Review

By: Derek, age 9
Grayslake, IL

I liked the Maelstrom ride a lot, but I could have skipped the movie after it. My favorite part of the ride was when the troll curses your boat and you almost fall backward over a waterfall!

Who am I?

- I work at Number 17, Cherry Tree Lane.
- Bert's my buddy.
- I'm practically perfect in every way.

Answer: Mary Poppins

HoT TiP

Don't miss the special entertainment in each of the countries!

Epcot

Hidden Mickey Alert!

The volcano at the beginning of the boat ride is about to erupt! Watch the swirling smoke carefully and you might spot that famous mouse.

MEXICO

The pyramid-shaped building at the Mexico pavilion is home to a new attraction—Gran Fiesta Tour Starring the Three Caballeros. It is a boat trip that takes you through the country of Mexico.

The Three Caballeros are José, Panchito, and Donald (Duck, that is). They starred in a movie together way back in 1944. Now they're back together and planning to do a big show in Mexico City. But there is a problem. Donald keeps getting lost!

Don't worry, there is a happy ending. This is Disney World, after all! "Hello" here is *hola* (say: *OH-lah*).

The Reader Review

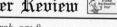

By: Sarah, age 8
Woodmere, NY

After a busy day at Epcot, the slow boat ride in Mexico is the perfect way to relax. During the ride you travel around a big volcano, and see Mexican shops and fireworks!

Entertainment

Epcot is known for its great entertainment. There are lots of shows and special performances every day of the year. For more information, check a park Times Guide.

ILLUMINATIONS: REFLECTIONS OF EARTH

An amazing fireworks show takes place each night on and around World Showcase Lagoon. It tells a story of Earth's creation. You can get a good view of it from anywhere around the lagoon.

JAMMITORS

One of the loudest and wildest shows is inside Future World, where musicians bang out rhythms on trash cans and, sometimes, on one another.

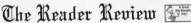

The Reader Review

By: Jordan, age 14
Maynard, MA

Illuminations is absolutely beautiful. It's a great way of telling the story of Earth's creation. You can get a good view from anywhere around the lagoon, but I like to watch from the United Kingdom.

WORLD SHOWCASE PERFORMERS

There is some form of entertainment at each of the pavilions in World Showcase. Some of the highlights include acrobats in France, the Voices of Liberty at the American Adventure, and the British Invasion in the United Kingdom. The British Invasion is a funky band that sounds like the Beatles. The Voices of Liberty sing patriotic songs. Feel free to sing along!

Where to find
CHARACTERS
at EPCOT

The best place to meet characters is at the Epcot Character Connection in **Innoventions West** in Future World. Different characters take turns hanging out here, so you never know who you might see. One thing you can be sure of: They will always be happy to sign autographs and pose for photos.

You may also run into characters from classic Disney films while wandering around **World Showcase**. They usually show up during the afternoon hours. Don't forget to ask the characters to sign the autograph section of this book!

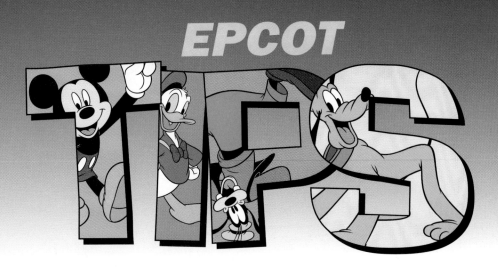

EPCOT TIPS

Start your day early at Soarin', followed by Test Track, and the "less intense" version of Mission: SPACE. Then stop in to say hi to Nemo at The Seas with Nemo & Friends. After that, head over to the Imagination pavilion.

Remember: World Showcase doesn't open until 11 A.M.

Need a refreshing splash? Visit Cool Wash by Test Track, the squirting sidewalk that leads to World Showcase, or the fountain by Mission: SPACE.

Check the electronic Tip Board in Innoventions Plaza. It lets you know how long the wait is for many attractions.

There is a special garbage can in the Electric Umbrella restaurant and a special drinking fountain near The Land pavilion. Why are they special? They talk!

Innoventions is very big and can be tiring. Visit this pavilion early in the day or after a meal, when you are rested and full of energy.

Bring pins with you so you'll have something to trade with other guests at the pin trading booth in Future World. (Get a parent's permission before you trade anything.)

Try not to squeeze the movies at Canada, France, and China all into one day.

Take time to talk to the people who work in World Showcase. Most of them come from the country of the pavilion they represent, and they have many interesting stories to tell.

You can sample soda for free at Club Cool. It's in Future World (near Innoventions).

Epcot

Attraction Ratings

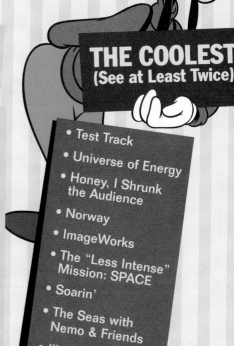

COOL
(Check It Out)

- The Circle of Life
- China
- Italy
- United Kingdom
- Morocco
- Germany
- Japan
- Spaceship Earth

REALLY COOL
(Don't Miss)

- The American Adventure
- Journey Into Imagination with Figment
- Innoventions
- Gran Fiesta Tour
- France
- Canada
- Living with the Land
- Mexico
- Universe of Energy

THE COOLEST
(See at Least Twice)

- Test Track
- Universe of Energy
- Honey, I Shrunk the Audience
- Norway
- ImageWorks
- The "Less Intense" Mission: SPACE
- Soarin'
- The Seas with Nemo & Friends
- IllumiNations

Epcot

Your favorite Epcot attractions

Disney-MGM Studios

The Disney-MGM Studios lets you see some of the magic of making movies and TV shows. There are attractions that show how animation is done, how sound effects are made, how stunts are performed, and lots more.

The Studios looks a little like Hollywood did back in the 1940s. Hollywood is the California city where movie-making got its big start. The Disney-MGM Studios got its big start in 1989. Since then, lots of famous movies and TV shows have been made there. A crew might even be filming something when you are visiting.

One of the best things about this park is that you can be a part of some attractions. It's fun to be right in the middle of the action, so be sure to volunteer. You will also get to meet a ton of characters, including the stars of some of Disney's recent animated hits—so remember to bring a pen for their autographs.

Use this map to explore the Disney-MGM Studios theme park.

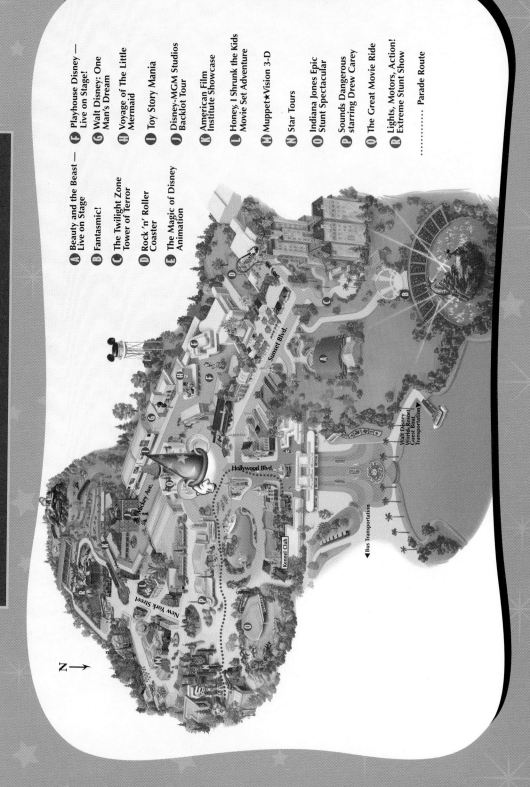

- **A** Beauty and the Beast — Live on Stage!
- **B** Fantasmic!
- **C** The Twilight Zone Tower of Terror
- **D** Rock 'n' Roller Coaster
- **E** The Magic of Disney Animation
- **F** Playhouse Disney — Live on Stage!
- **G** Walt Disney: One Man's Dream
- **H** Voyage of The Little Mermaid
- **I** Toy Story Mania
- **J** Disney-MGM Studios Backlot Tour
- **K** American Film Institute Showcase
- **L** Honey, I Shrunk the Kids Movie Set Adventure
- **M** Muppet★Vision 3-D
- **N** Star Tours
- **O** Indiana Jones Epic Stunt Spectacular
- **P** Sounds Dangerous starring Drew Carey
- **Q** The Great Movie Ride
- **R** Lights, Motors, Action! Extreme Stunt Show
- ·········· Parade Route

Sunset Blvd.

Hollywood Blvd.

Mickey Ave.

New York Street

Kennel Club

▶Bus Transportation

Walt Disney World Resort Guest Boat Transportation▶

N →

HoT TiP If you need something to hold onto while riding Tower, grab the handle beside your seat!

The Twilight Zone™ Tower of Terror

READER #5 RIDE PLEASER

The HOLLYWOOD TOWER Hotel

At a height of 199 feet, Tower of Terror is one of the tallest attractions at Walt Disney World. For some people, it's also the scariest.

Legend says that one Halloween night, lightning hit The Hollywood Tower Hotel. A whole section of the hotel disappeared! So did an elevator carrying five people. No one ever saw them again.

Now the hotel is haunted. If you dare to enter it, you are in for a few surprises. First, you walk through the dusty hotel lobby. Then you enter a tiny room, where Rod Serling appears on TV. (He was the star of a sometimes scary show called *The Twilight Zone*.) Once Rod tells you the story of The Hollywood Tower Hotel, get ready—you are on your way to the Twilight Zone.

Going down!

After waiting in the boiler room for a little while, you are given a seat in a big elevator. The elevator ride takes you on a short tour of the hotel, where you see many special effects. But the highlight comes when the elevator cables snap. *Whoosh!* You plunge eight stories! Next the elevator shoots up to the hotel's 13th floor. It teeters for a moment and then ... it drops again and again at blazing speed!

A thrilling experience

People who love thrills think this is a great ride. And now it's even more suspenseful because you never know how many times the elevator will drop. Sometimes it feels like you'll be trapped in the Twilight Zone forever.

You must be at least 40 inches tall to ride—and very brave!

Disney-MGM Studios

83

Rock 'n' Roller Coaster starring Aerosmith

This ride rocks! It travels at top speed and flips you upside down three times. It also has a rock 'n' roll sound track that will have you dancing in your seat.

You're invited

Rock 'n' Roller Coaster goes really fast—it takes you from zero to 60 miles per hour in the first three seconds of the ride! You need the speed because you're on your way to a party at an Aerosmith concert—and you're running late.

It's showtime!

The ride takes place in a limousine on a roller coaster track. The limousine's radio is tuned to the Aerosmith concert. You can hear the band warming up, but your car is not moving yet. Then, just as the concert starts, the light turns green and you're on your way. You zoom along the California highway and make it just in time for the end of the show. Hang on!

You must be at least 48 inches tall to ride Rock 'n' Roller Coaster.

The Reader Review

By: Kate, age 13
Sewell, NJ

Woo-hoo! This is the best roller coaster in all of Disney World. I like it because it goes really fast and I like the music.

Beauty and the Beast—Live on Stage

It's hard to keep quiet during this stage show—it makes you want to clap and sing along. The music comes straight from Disney's animated film *Beauty and the Beast*.

As the show begins, Belle is frustrated by life in her small town. She is dreaming of exciting, faraway places. Later on, she becomes a prisoner in the Beast's castle. All of the castle's residents are under a magic spell! Lumiere, Cogsworth, Mrs. Potts, and the rest of the gang are there to help Belle (and perform "Be Our Guest"). In the end, the spell is broken. The Beast becomes human again.

The show is performed several days a week. Read a park Times Guide for schedules and dates. You can get a free guide in most shops in the park. Just ask.

The Reader Review

A Great Big Beautiful Day!

By: Pharra, age 11
Alpharetta, GA

I liked the lively colors and the music in this show. I didn't like how it skipped so fast from one song to the next, because that made it more challenging to follow along, but I still got the story. It's a show the entire family can enjoy!

Hidden Mickey Alert!

Mickey and pals are drawn on the Well of Souls. Look for them on the wall during the Indiana Jones scene.

The Great Movie Ride

How many movies have you seen in your lifetime? Hundreds? Thousands? Well, how many have you actually been in? Probably not too many! This attraction lets you ride through scenes from several old movies.

Pay attention!

First, you'll watch short clips from famous films. Pay close attention—these are the scenes that you will visit later on.

As you enter the ride vehicle, take time to look around. The room is set up like a movie set (a stage where movie scenes are filmed). The background looks like the hills of Hollywood. That's the California town where movie-making got its big start.

A trip to Munchkinland

Once the car starts moving, you'll pass through scenes from movies like *Mary Poppins*, *Alien*, and *Fantasia*. One of the best scenes is straight out of *The Wizard of Oz*. It looks just like Munchkinland! (Beware: The Wicked Witch of the West pops in for a visit.)

The Reader Review

By: Philip, age 12
Glen Carbon, IL

I am not really a fan of old movies, but I loved this ride. I felt like I was in the movie scenes. The best part was when the tour guide got kidnapped. I sat by my grandma, and since she loves movies, this ride was a big hit for her, too!

The Magic of Disney Animation

Anybody can create a cartoon character. All you need is a pencil, some paper, and a little imagination. But how do you get that character to *move*? That's where the animation part comes in.

This attraction shows you how *Tarzan*, *Lilo and Stitch*, and other animated movies were made. In the

waiting area, there are drawings on the walls. Later, you'll find out how artists called *animators* bring these kinds of sketches to life.

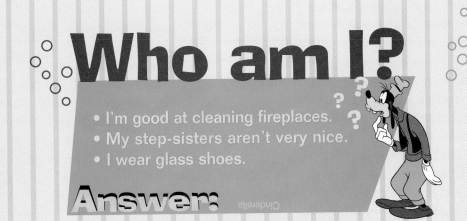

Who am I?

- I'm good at cleaning fireplaces.
- My step-sisters aren't very nice.
- I wear glass shoes.

Answer: Cinderella

Hidden Mickey Alert!
Lasers at the start of the show form a Mickey head.

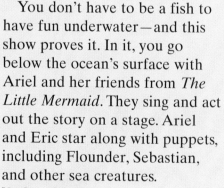

SCARY
Attraction Reaction

LOUD
Attraction Reaction

DARK
Attraction Reaction

Voyage of The Little Mermaid

You don't have to be a fish to have fun underwater—and this show proves it. In it, you go below the ocean's surface with Ariel and her friends from *The Little Mermaid*. They sing and act out the story on a stage. Ariel and Eric star along with puppets, including Flounder, Sebastian, and other sea creatures.

Under the sea

There are some great special effects that draw you into the show. A screen of water makes it seem like the theater really is under the sea. Lasers flash, lightning strikes, and mist sprays the audience. Scenes from the movie are shown on a big screen behind the stage.

A winning combination

The combination of people, puppets, and special effects makes for a terrific show. To get the best view of all the action, try sitting toward the back of the theater. From there, the puppets look like they are really swimming!

Playhouse Disney—Live on Stage!

Do you know how to do the cha-cha? Well, Bear does, and he'll be happy to show you how in this musical stage show. Lots of Bear's Disney Channel friends are along for the performance, too (characters from *The Book of Pooh*, *JoJo's Circus*, and *Little Einsteins*). So if you're a fan of Playhouse Disney, you're sure to have a good time.

Home, sweet home

When you walk into the auditorium, you'll notice something unusual about it—there are no seats. But don't worry. The carpet is comfy, so sit down and make yourself at home. Soon the gang will sing and dance, and have lots of fun.

A big hit with little guests

Big kids may get a kick out of Playhouse Disney—Live On Stage!, but little kids seem to have the most fun here. If you have younger brothers or sisters, be sure to bring them to this show!

HoT TiP

This show is very popular with little kids. Check show times and be sure to arrive early.

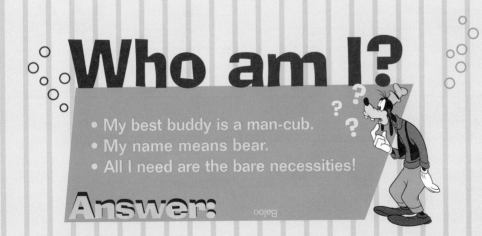

Who am I?

- My best buddy is a man-cub.
- My name means bear.
- All I need are the bare necessities!

Answer: Baloo

Toy Story Mania

If you think Buzz Lightyear's Space Ranger Spin is a blast, you will love Toy Story Mania. It's like jumping into a life-size computer game. It also makes you feel like you're the size of a toy as you travel through some super colorful rooms—all while aiming your laser cannon at cool targets.

Of course, this new ride has a new twist: all guests wear 3-D glasses. That makes all of the special effects really pop. As you rack up points, you'll be cheered on by Woody, Buzz, Hamm, and other *Toy Story* stars.

This attraction is good for gamers of all ages and skill levels. So if you are a beginner, don't worry. You'll get better every time you play. In fact, we're pretty sure you'll be giving pointers to your parents!

Toy Story Mania should be open by the fall of 2008.

HOT TIP The attraction called Who Wants to Be a Millionaire —Play It! closed in 2006.

Lights, Motors, Action! Extreme Stunt Show

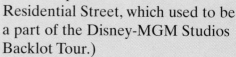

High-speed car chases, loud crashes, and giant splashes happen in lots of movies and TV shows. Of course, they are all staged by experts who fool you into thinking all the action is real and sometimes dangerous. This stunt show has all of the above, plus a whole lot more in-your-face action. It gives guests a behind-the-scenes look at how the folks in Hollywood make amazing stunts seem so realistic.

This stunt show is staged in an area beyond the Honey, I Shrunk the Kids Movie Set Adventure. (It takes the place of Residential Street, which used to be a part of the Disney-MGM Studios Backlot Tour.)

Many kids think this is a very exciting show. But it can be a little scary, too—especially when it seems like a stunt-person is on fire. Don't worry, it's all part of the show. If you don't like fire or loud noises, grab a seat in the back of the theater. It's less intense back there.

PHOTO BY JILL SAFRO

READER TIP

"Ponchos aren't just handy when it rains. They're great for rides that get you wet, too!"

Amy (age 11)
New Castle, PA

LOUD
Attraction Reaction

Disney-MGM Studios

Disney-MGM Studios Backlot Tour

There's a real working film studio inside this theme park. A tram ride lets you see parts of the backstage areas where movies and TV shows have been created. You also get an inside peek at the secrets behind some special effects.

Very special effects

The first stop on the tour is beside a big pool of water. There's a little boat and a human host. Your host shows you how filmmakers can take a sunny theme park day and turn it into a dark, stormy day at sea. You'll also learn how a little toy battle can seem real with a little bit of movie-making know-how.

A grand canyon

The trip includes a stop at Catastrophe Canyon—a special-effects area. Here you see a fire and a flash flood. (You may get a little bit wet.) The tram also takes you through the costume department, and past props from famous movies.

The Reader Review

A Great
Big Beautiful
Day!

By: Abbey, age 10
Pepper Pike, OH

The tour is good for people who want to learn about movie-making. It's sort of slow, so if you are in the mood for speedy stuff, it's not for you.

Disney-MGM Studios

Honey, I Shrunk the Kids Movie Set Adventure

The backyard from the *Honey, I Shrunk the Kids* movie has been re-created as a big playground. Even grown-ups feel small here. There are 30-foot blades of grass, a huge water gun, a giant toy truck, and more. There are things to climb on, slide down, and explore.

Most kids enjoy getting wet under the leaky garden hose. Nobody stays dry!

It's a great way to cool off after all that running and climbing.

The Reader Review

By: Marcelo, age 6
Coral Gables, FL

You feel as small as an ant in this giant backyard. And there's so much to do! There's a huge spiderweb to climb, and tree roots that you can step on to make music. It's lots of fun!

Who am I?

- We are related.
- We aren't human.
- Mickey Mouse is our uncle.

Answer: Morty and Ferdie

Hidden Mickey Alert!

The Muppets have made some Hidden Mickeys of their own! Look on their building for funny eyes and noses that together form the shape of Mickey heads.

READER TIP

"Don't rush to be the first one in the theater—you'll have to sit at the end of your row, and the view is better from the middle."

David (age 14)
Calabasas, CA

Disney-MGM Studios

Muppet*Vision 3-D

Don't miss this attraction—it's one of Walt Disney World's best. It begins with a funny pre-show starring Fozzie Bear, Gonzo, Scooter, and Sam Eagle. Then you go into a special theater that looks just like the one from Jim Henson's *The Muppet Show*. Here, you see 3-D movie effects mixed with some other special tricks.

Amazing effects

Some of the effects are so good that it's hard to tell what's part of the movie and what's real. During Miss Piggy's big song, bubbles look like they are just inches away from you. Don't be surprised if they really are!

Look around the theater

Be sure to look all around you when you're watching the show. Some of the best action happens off the screen. Try to keep an eye out for the Swedish Chef. He's cooking up a plan in the back of the theater!

The Reader Review

A Great Big Beautiful Day!

By: Carrie, age 13
Hinsdale, IL

This is an all-around great show. I recommend it to everyone! The characters in the movie come right out at you, and you feel like you could reach out and touch them. It's very cool!

Hidden Mickey Alert!

Mickey is hiding on the phone directory sign by the entrance. Can you spot him?

READER TIP

"Star Tours really pulls you around and shakes you up. Be prepared for a wild ride!"

Kinsey (age 7)
Athens, GA

Disney-MGM Studios

Star Tours

Soar through the galaxy on an out-of-control spaceship and experience the thrills of the movie *Star Wars*. Your pilot is Captain Rex. He's new on the job and can't seem to find his way through all the giant ice crystals and other spaceships.

It feels real

This ride takes place on a flight simulator, the same type used to train astronauts and pilots. The combination of the simulator and the movie makes you feel like you're really rocketing through outer space.

Rex is a rotten pilot

The pilot keeps going the wrong way, but that's what makes the trip so exciting. His sharp turns make the ride really bumpy and rough.

You must be at least 40 inches tall to experience Star Tours.

Hot Tip

If you start to feel dizzy on Star Tours, just close your eyes or look down at the floor to feel better.

94

Walt Disney: One Man's Dream

You probably know a lot about Mickey Mouse—he has a pup named Pluto, he loves red shorts, and Minnie's his favorite gal. But how much do you know about the man who created him? You can learn a lot about Walt Disney at this attraction. He's the man who started the Walt Disney Company.

Take your time

Lots of Walt's belongings are on display in the pre-show area. Look for special items like old family photos, his piano, and the Academy Award he won for *Snow White and the Seven Dwarfs*. Spend some time exploring the exhibits before you see the movie.

Fun fact

Did you know that Mickey Mouse wasn't Walt's first famous cartoon character? A rabbit named Oswald was. But Walt's plans for Oswald didn't quite work out. Luckily, he never gave up, or he wouldn't have created Mickey!

To learn more about Walt Disney, turn to page 8 of this book.

The Reader Review

By: Jennifer, age 12
Salina, KS

This is a wonderful attraction. It really helps you get to know Walt Disney and the magic he brought to the world.

HoT TiP

If you want to meet the characters from Toy Story, visit Al's Toy Barn.

Toy Story Pizza Planet Arcade

This arcade and restaurant looks a little like Andy's favorite pizza place from the movie *Toy Story*. It's located near Muppet*Vision 3-D. If you have trouble finding it, just look for the giant Mr. Potato Head and Rex the Dinosaur sitting on top of the building. Inside are lots of "claw" prize machines and video games, plus a fast-food counter with pizza, salad, juice boxes, and other snacks.

Who am I?

- I have bad manners.
- I am cursed.
- Don't touch my flower!

Answer: Beast

READER TIP

"Sit toward the front of the theater to get the best view of the effects."
Shawn (age 10)
Burbank, OH

Indiana Jones Epic Stunt Spectacular

Fire, explosions, daring escapes, and other special effects are the stars of this attraction. Stuntmen and stuntwomen act out scenes from the movie *Raiders of the Lost Ark* and show how special effects are done. The audience watches from a large theater, and adults are chosen to perform with the pros. (It's too dangerous for kids.)

Fun for everyone

All the surprises keep everyone on the edge of their seats. One of the best parts of the show is the re-creation of the scene in the movie where the giant ball rolls down and seems to crush Indiana Jones. Even though you know it's a stunt, it looks so real!

Don't try this at home

Stunt people act out the scenes and then explain how each of the stunts was performed. They make it look easy, but it isn't!

The Reader Review

By: Ellen, age 15
Gibbsboro, NJ

This show is every bit as exciting as the Indiana Jones movies. The show is loud, but not scary, because everything is under control.

HoT TiP

After the show, visit the area by the exit called **Sound Works,** for some do-it-yourself sound effects.

Sounds Dangerous Starring Drew Carey

You may have seen a 3-D movie before, but have you ever seen a movie with 3-D sound? For this one, you have to wear special headphones that make the action sound like it's happening all around you.

Inspector Carey

Drew Carey is the hero of this funny film. He's supposed to be an actor whose character is an undercover detective. But the detective is not very good at his job. And he's wearing a camera, so the audience can see (and hear) all the mistakes he makes.

Drew sneaks into a warehouse to spy on some jewel smugglers. When he runs into a security guard, he panics—and hides the camera in his mouth (which breaks it, of course).

Lights out!

The next thing you know, the theater is dark and you can only hear what's going on through your headphones. The sounds seem so real that the action is easy to follow.

The Reader Review

By: Kyle, age 14
Contoocook, NH

This may be scary for little kids. It's pitch dark and the sounds are loud. Plus, you might get too nervous when it sounds like the magician is throwing knives at you!

Entertainment

Lights! Camera! Action! There's a lot of star-studded entertainment at the Disney-MGM Studios. Most of it has a TV or movie theme. Two of the best shows are described below.

HIGH SCHOOL MUSICAL PEP RALLY

Get'cha whole body in the game at this lively, interactive show. Presented in front of the giant sorcerer's hat, this peppy performance includes hit songs from the ever-popular *High School Musical* movie. Be prepared to sing and dance along with the cast. You may even get to shoot some hoops!

FANTASMIC!

What does Mickey Mouse dream about? You can find out at Fantasmic! It's an amazing show that combines laser lights, Disney characters, movies, music, and a little magic.

Mickey's dreams are fun to watch—but some of them are a little scary. (Disney villains keep turning his dreams into nightmares.) In the end, good wins over evil and Mickey's dreams are happy once more.

Fantasmic! is presented nightly in a theater behind The Twilight Zone Tower of Terror attraction. It's very popular, so be sure to line up at least an hour before the show starts. And, if it isn't summer, bring a jacket or a sweater—it can get chilly! If you sit near the front, you might get a little bit wet. The water gets lit on fire, too. Just a warning.

BLOCK PARTY BASH

This new parade has a special twist: It stops moving and a few times and the performers put on show! It's led by the Green Army Men from *Toy Story*. They are joined by lots of Disney characters, plus acrobats, dancers, and more. It happens once a day. Check a park Times Guide for the schedule.

Where to find
CHARACTERS
at the Disney-MGM Studios

There are lots of places to meet Disney characters at the Studios. One of the best spots is the **Streets of America**. Characters such as Kim Possible, the Power Rangers, Mater, and Lightning McQueen stop by all day. You can get a ton of pictures!

Where's Mickey? Good question! He tends to pop up in places all over the park. Ask a cast member or check a guidemap to find out where he'll be during your visit, so you can stop by and say hello!

Buzz, Woody, and Jessie from *Toy Story* have their very own spot for meeting guests. You can pose for pictures with them in front of **Al's Toy Barn** near New York Street. Ask them to sign the autograph section at the end of this book!

DISNEY-MGM STUDIOS

Arrive at the Disney-MGM Studios before the opening time. The gates often open a few minutes ahead of the scheduled time.

Bring this book to the park. When you run into characters, you'll have something for them to sign!

There are "chicken exits" at both Tower of Terror and Rock 'n' Roller Coaster, just in case you change your mind at the last minute.

Don't eat a thing for at least an hour before you ride Rock 'n' Roller Coaster or the Twilight Zone Tower of Terror.

Some stage shows don't open until late morning. Be sure to check a Times Guide for exact showtimes.

To get a good spot to see the afternoon parade, line up on Hollywood Boulevard about 30 minutes early.

The Streets of America area is a good place to meet characters.

The front rows at Fantasmic! get a little wet. The best seats are in the back at either end of the theater.

See Tower of Terror and Rock 'n' Roller Coaster in the morning, before the lines get too long. Get a Fastpass if you can!

Attraction Ratings

Disney-MGM Studios

COOL
(Check It Out)

- The Great Movie Ride
- Honey, I Shrunk the Kids Movie Set Adventure
- Playhouse Disney—Live on Stage!
- Walt Disney: One Man's Dream

REALLY COOL
(Don't Miss)

- Indiana Jones Epic Stunt Spectacular
- Disney-MGM Studios Backlot Tour
- Disney Stars and Motor Cars Parade
- Fantasmic!
- Sounds Dangerous starring Drew Carey
- Lights, Motors, Action! Extreme Stunt Show

THE COOLEST
(See at Least Twice)

- Muppet*Vision 3-D
- Star Tours
- The Twilight Zone Tower of Terror
- Beauty and the Beast —Live on Stage
- The Magic of Disney Animation
- Voyage of The Little Mermaid
- Rock 'n' Roller Coaster
- Toy Story Mania

Your favorite Disney-MGM Studios attractions

Disney's Animal Kingdom

The newest park in Walt Disney World is called Animal Kingdom. It celebrates animals of every kind, from lions, tigers, and zebras to giant turtles whose ancestors lived during the time of the dinosaurs. And they're all real! You may get closer to them than you've ever been before. There are dinosaurs, too. The dinos aren't real, but they sure seem to be.

Animal Kingdom is a theme park with many attractions. Just like at the Magic Kingdom, there are different "lands" to visit in Animal Kingdom. The major lands are called Discovery Island, DinoLand U.S.A., Asia, Africa, and Camp Minnie-Mickey.

You enter the park through The Oasis. It's a big garden with plants and animals. Take some time to look around. Then cross a bridge to Discovery Island, admire the giant Tree of Life, and decide which land to explore first.

What's the best way to see Animal Kingdom? Use this map to help you decide!

ASIA

I Flights of Wonder at Caravan Stage

J Maharajah Jungle Trek

K Kali River Rapids

L Expedition Everest

DINOLAND U.S.A.

M Dinosaur

N The Boneyard playground

O Finding Nemo—The Musical

P Chester & Hester's Dino-Rama!

AFRICA

A Kilimanjaro Safaris

B Pangani Forest Exploration Trail

C Wildlife Express to Rafiki's Planet Watch

D Rafiki's Planet Watch

DISCOVERY ISLAND

E The Tree of Life

F Discovery Island Trails

G It's Tough to be a Bug!

CAMP MINNIE-MICKEY

H Festival of the Lion King

Discovery Island

Discovery Island is the gateway to all the other lands in the park. (It used to be called Safari Village.) The Tree of Life stands near the center of Discovery Island. If you wander around its roots, you'll see all kinds of animals.

Hidden Mickey Alert!

There's a mouse in the moss! Look for clusters of moss near the tiger. They form a Hidden Mickey.

The Tree of Life

This man-made tree is 145 feet tall. From far away it looks like any other tree. But when you get up close, you'll realize that this is not an ordinary tree. It's covered with animals!

Artists have carved 325 animal images into its trunk. In fact, it's called The Tree of Life because it's covered with so many different kinds of animal life. The lion is easy to see. Other animals, such as the ant and dolphin, are a lot harder to spot. How many can you find?

The Reader Review

By: John, age 14
Washington Township, NJ

Once inside Animal Kingdom, you can't miss The Tree of Life. Trying to spot all the animals on the tree is nearly impossible! A great place to search for animals is while in line for It's Tough to be a Bug!

HoT TiP

If you hate creepy crawlers, skip It's Tough to be a Bug!

It's Tough to be a Bug!

 Disney's **FASTPASS**

 SCARY — Attraction Reaction

 LOUD — Attraction Reaction

 DARK — Attraction Reaction

The Tree of Life has a hollow trunk. It's cool, dark, and roomy inside. That makes it a great place to watch a 3-D movie called It's Tough to be a Bug! It's hosted by Flik, the star of *A Bug's Life*. Most of these bugs are friendly and funny. But when Flik's enemy Hopper makes an appearance, the show gets a little bit scary.

This movie is about the tiny creatures that outnumber all others on our planet—bugs. In it, animated insects use music and special effects to show how hard their lives are. They also try to show humans just how important bugs really are.

The Reader Review

 A Great Big Beautiful Day!

By: Benjamin, age 11
East Providence, RI

I am not a big fan of insects, so I found this show very suspenseful. You never know where the bugs are going to pop up next! The effects are great, right down to the Audio-Animatronics Flik and Hopper.

DinoLand U.S.A.

The entrance to this land is marked by a big dinosaur skeleton. Inside, you will find life-like dinosaurs as well as live animals that have existed since prehistoric times. The main attraction is Dinosaur, but there are lots of other things to see and do. For a hand-clapping good time, catch Finding Nemo—The Musical. In DinoLand you can also dig for bones in an amazing playground, learn about real dinosaurs, or take a spin on a friendly dino ride.

Chester & Hester's Dino-Rama!

 Disney's **FASTPASS**

 ROUGH Attraction Reaction

The newest area of Animal Kingdom is this wacky section of DinoLand U.S.A. It's a dino-themed fair complete with carnival games and two thrilling little rides.

TriceraTop Spin

The dinos that soar on this ride look like they're part of an antique wind-up toy. Just like at Dumbo the Flying Elephant, riders here can control how high or low their TriceraTops go.

Primeval Whirl

Speedy little cars race around the track on this mini roller coaster. Each car spins as it moves, which makes for an even wilder trip. You must be at least 48 inches tall to ride.

The Reader Review

 A Great Big Beautiful Day!

By: Jessilyn, age 13
Billings, MT

Primeval Whirl has sharp turns and quick drops. You are always wondering what's next. It's small, but it is a thriller. If you're afraid of heights or drops, you probably should not ride this one.

Dinosaur

This thrilling ride takes guests back to the last few minutes of the Cretaceous Period. (That's when the dinosaurs died out.) Kids who have been to Animal Kingdom before may remember the ride by its old name—Countdown to Extinction.

Save the dinosaur

The mission on Dinosaur is to save the last iguanodon. You have to brave a meteor shower and the largest Audio-Animatronics

creature Disney has ever made. It's a dinosaur called a carnotaurus, and it may be the ugliest thing you've ever seen. This monster has the face of a toad, horns like a bull, and squirrel-like arms. It looks like it's alive. The nostrils even move as it breathes. And, boy, can it run. The carnotaurus runs for about 30 feet. Be careful! This hungry monster is not just after the iguanodon—it wants to eat *you*, too.

An exciting (and scary) ride

Most kids agree that this is a very exciting ride, but one that might not be for everyone. Kids who don't like scary rides can find some tamer dinos on TriceraTop Spin. But for kids who like to be scared, Dinosaur is a must.

You must be at least 40 inches tall to ride Dinosaur.

The Reader Review

By: Samantha, age 13
Churubusco, IN

I love Dinosaur! The dinosaurs, darkness, and roughness make the ride extra exciting. It only lasts a few minutes, but it seemed a lot longer to me. If you like rough rides, this is one of the roughest!

READER TIP

"Dinosaur is very loud and dark, and it really jerks and pulls you around. Some young kids won't like it at all!"

Julia (age 11)
Prairieville, LA

Finding Nemo— The Musical

Uh-oh. Nemo has wandered off *again*. Will he never learn?! We hope not, since this show tells his story in a whole new way—with music! There's lots of peppy tunes to sing along with during the performance. High-flying acrobats, colorful (gigantic) puppets, and talented dancers round out the show.

The action takes place in DinoLand's Theater in the Wild. The show happens in a building, but it seems like it's under water. You won't get wet, though, since it's all done with special effects. The 30-minute musical is presented several times a day. Check a Times Guide for the schedule. It's a popular show—arrive early. The theater is air-conditioned, so you can cool off while Nemo and friends entertain.

The Boneyard

Are you ready to jump into the biggest sandbox you've ever seen? It's here, and it's filled with bones! You can uncover the bones of a mammoth and find clues about how the animal died.

There are also dinosaur footprints that roar when you jump in them, and a xylophone that's made of dinosaur bones. There's a rope maze for climbing and plenty of slippery slides, too. Be sure to check out the OldenGate Bridge. It's made from a huge dinosaur skeleton.

Hot Tip

The xylophone is next to the trunk in The Boneyard playground. Press the bones to make music.

The Reader Review

By: Olivia, age 9
Watertown, WI

My brother is 5 years old and he had a better time at The Boneyard than I did. There's lots to do, but I couldn't wait to ride Dinosaur!

Africa

Before creating this land, Disney Imagineers spent months on the continent of Africa learning all about the plants and animals there. When they came back, they made an African forest and a grassland in Florida. Then they filled it with hundreds of the same animals they had seen in Africa. Most of the animals in Animal Kingdom came from special parks and zoos around the world. You can see many animals on a safari ride and learn all about them at Rafiki's Planet Watch.

Kilimanjaro Safaris

In this wild jungle adventure, you ride in a vehicle that's wide open. There's almost nothing between you and the animals! You may see hippos, lions, giraffes, rhinos, elephants, and more. Some animals may even come up close. But don't worry—the dangerous animals can't get near you.

After a calm sightseeing tour, the ride takes a different twist. There are poachers hunting for elephants, and the animals need your help. The safari ride ends with a wild chase over muddy roads to catch the bad guys.

The Reader Review

By: Jennifer, age 12
Mesquite, TX

It really felt like we were in Africa! This safari ride is a great way to see animals up close. My favorites were the lions and zebras. During our trip, a baby giraffe came right up to our car!

Pangani Forest Exploration Trail

After you take a ride on the Kilimanjaro Safaris, go for a walk on the Pangani Forest Exploration Trail. This nature trail is filled with many exciting sights. You'll come nose-to-nose with a naked mole rat and look for hippos underwater. Exotic fish and birds live in the African Aviary.

No binoculars necessary

Pick up a bird guide (they should be hanging on a post in the aviary) and see how many different birds you can spot. Afterward, make a stop at the meerkat exhibit. Some people call it the "Timon exhibit" because he's a meerkat. (There are no Pumbaas here, though. Meerkats and warthogs don't get along in real life.)

Greetings, gorillas

At the end of the trail, you see a family of gorillas. They are usually hanging out on the hills or playing. You might even spot a baby gorilla in the group.

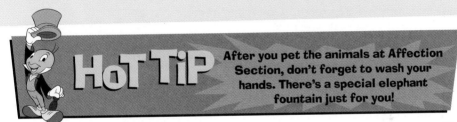

HoT TiP After you pet the animals at Affection Section, don't forget to wash your hands. There's a special elephant fountain just for you!

Rafiki's Planet Watch

A train called the Wildlife Express is the only way to get to Rafiki's Planet Watch. (Hop aboard in Africa.) During the ride, you get a behind-the-scenes look at the buildings where animals from the safari ride are cared for.

Lend a helping hand

The exhibits at Rafiki's Planet Watch teach you what animals need to survive—and what people can do to help. There is an animal hospital, places for baby animals to get special care, and lots of shows meant to get you excited about conservation. There are even ways to find out about some conservation projects near your home. It's also a great place to meet Disney characters.

Talk to the animals

Many exhibits at Rafiki's Planet Watch are interactive. In Song of the Rain Forest, you're surrounded by sounds you might hear in a real rain forest. At the Hallway of Animal Health and Care, you can sometimes watch doctors care for animals. People can walk among animals like goats and sheep in the Affection Section. Go ahead and pet them, but remember: Feeding is not allowed.

Asia

Asia is the largest continent on Earth. It's almost twice as big as North America! The land called Asia in Animal Kingdom is a lot smaller than the real thing, but gives you an idea of what the Asian continent is like. It has jungles and rain forests and magnificent animals. It's also home to the fastest raging river in Animal Kingdom. If you want to get wet, you can shoot the rapids down the river on a ride called Kali River Rapids. And for one of the most exciting experiences of all, ride Expedition Everest! For a calmer experience, make a trip to the Caravan Stage.

Maharajah Jungle Trek

Put on your walking shoes and keep your eyes peeled. This jungle trail is the place to spot strange, scaly animals called Komodo dragons, deer, giant fruit bats (they snack on melon), and lots of tigers. You'll also see many colorful birds along the way and tons of plants and trees. Pick up a map at the beginning of the trail to know what to look for.

You see the bats about halfway through your walk. Their wings are enormous! In some places, there's no glass between you and the bats. But don't worry—they're not interested in humans. Still, it might be creepy to stand so close to them. If the bats make you uncomfortable, there's a window outside the building that lets you observe them from a distance.

Hidden Mickey Alert!
The mural by the tigers is where this Mickey head is hiding!

READER #3 RIDE PLEASER

READER TIP

"Remember to bring a water bottle with you to Animal Kingdom on hot days."
Meg (age 12)
Vero Beach, FL

Expedition Everest

Disney's FASTPASS

DARK Attraction Reaction

SCARY Attraction Reaction

ROUGH Attraction Reaction

Mount Everest is the tallest mountain in the world. Can you guess the name of the tallest mountain in Walt Disney World? If you said Expedition Everest, you're right! Of course, it is much more than a mountain. It's a thrilling new train ride through forests and waterfalls, and over snowcapped mountain peaks. This train ride is a lot rougher than Big Thunder Mountain. Here, you not only travel forward and backward through caverns and canyons, you also come face-to-face with an angry yeti (that's an abominable snowman). His job is to protect the mountain from you!

This attraction is not for everyone. If you love wild, crazy, dark, and SCARY rides—and are at least 44 inches tall—give it a try. And be sure to say hello to the yeti for us!

The Reader Review

By: Cameron, age 9
Naples, FL

I enjoy this fast-moving water ride. I really like the waterfall, but not the fire. It can scare some kids. It's fun when people shoot water at you, too.

Kali River Rapids

Disney's FASTPASS

WET — Attraction Reaction

ROUGH — Attraction Reaction

This is one of the wettest and wildest rides in Walt Disney World. Don't bother trying to pick a dry seat on the raft, because everyone gets wet! It begins as a peaceful raft trip through a rain forest. But things don't stay calm for very long. The raft bumps along down the river, spinning and turning every time it hits a rock.

Along the way you catch a glimpse of how logging (cutting down trees for lumber) can destroy the rain forest. Don't be scared if you see a fire raging out of control—that's just part of the ride. You avoid the burning logs, but will you be safe from the waterfall? We won't tell. (You might want to bring a towel, just in case!)

Guests must be at least 38 inches tall to ride the rapids.

Flights of Wonder

Live birds are the stars of this show that takes place on the Caravan Stage. They swoop and soar and do amazing tricks.

Sometimes one of the performers is an African gray parrot named Quasar. What is his special talent? He's a whiz at math!

This show is presented several times a day. Check a park Times Guide for the schedule. And get there early to snag a good seat!

Camp Minnie-Mickey

Disney characters have their very own vacation spot right here in Animal Kingdom. It's called Camp Minnie-Mickey, and it's a great place to meet characters like Mickey, Minnie, Goofy, and their friends. To find your favorite characters, just follow the trails through the forest. But save time to see the shows while you're here.

HoT TiP This is a great place to meet Disney characters. Don't forget your camera and something for them to autograph. (You can use this book!)

Festival of the Lion King

This is one spectacular musical show. Even if you have the movie memorized, you're in for a few surprises. Many of the major characters from the movie are here, but they look a little different. Most of them are played by humans dressed in colorful African costumes.

An action-packed performance

The theater has big stages that look like parade floats. (That's because they were once used in a parade at Disneyland!) On one, Simba sits atop Pride Rock. The wisecracking Pumbaa sits on another. Gymnasts dressed like monkeys use the center stage as a trampoline. They jump and do tricks.

The mighty jungle

After singers and dancers perform some of the most popular songs from *The Lion King*, it's time for the big finale. Stilt walkers, acrobats, and dancers all join the singers and characters for an exciting version of "The Lion Sleeps Tonight." Even the audience gets in on the act, so get ready to clap and sing along!

This is a very popular show. Check a park Times Guide for the schedule, and arrive at least 30 minutes before it starts.

Who am I?

- I'm a duck.
- My girlfriend shares a name with a flower.
- I often wear a sailor suit.

Answer: Donald

Pocahontas and Her Forest Friends

Who can save the forest? The wise old tree, Grandmother Willow, knows the answer. But she won't tell. She wants Pocahontas to figure it out all by herself.

This show is performed at Grandmother Willow's Grove. It takes you and Pocahontas on a journey through the forest. Together, you'll meet many different animals: rabbits, a raccoon, a skunk, and even a snake! And they are all real!

During the show, you will learn that every animal has its own special talent. You will also discover which animal can stop the forest from being destroyed.

This show is not performed every day of the week or at all times of the year. Check a park Times Guide to see if it is playing during your visit to the park.

Entertainment

Don't be surprised if the performers at Animal Kingdom come right up to you. Some walk on two legs, while others walk on four—or eight! There's a parade, plus street musicians, live animals, and many other things to entertain you along the way. Read all about them below.

AFRICAN ENTERTAINMENT

African music fills the air in the village of Harambe. Live bands perform here throughout the day. There's a covered area where you can listen to the music and escape the blazing sun.

HoT TiP

Animal Kingdom can get very hot—even hotter than the other theme parks. Be sure to drink lots of water!

MICKEY'S JAMMIN' JUNGLE PARADE

Mickey, Minnie, Goofy, and their character friends are on safari in this parade of jungle cars. There are also large animal puppets and peppy music to keep you singing and clapping along. Check a Times Guide for the parade time.

DISCOVERY ISLAND ENTERTAINMENT

In this land, storytellers tell animal tales while music based on sounds of nature plays in the background.

Where to find CHARACTERS at Disney's Animal Kingdom

It's easy to find Disney characters at Animal Kingdom—they have a land all their own. **Camp Minnie-Mickey** is the best place to meet characters in this park. Different characters hang out there all day. Ask them to sign the autograph section at the end of this book.

Of course, Camp Minnie-Mickey isn't the only place to find characters in Animal Kingdom. **Rafiki's Planet Watch** is a great place, too. Of course, Disney characters make appearances all over the park. So be on the lookout!

Donald Duck, Pluto, and other characters host breakfast at **Restaurantosaurus**.

Animal Kingdom

Animal Kingdom can get very hot, especially in the summer months. Head for Festival of the Lion King, Finding Nemo—The Musical, Kali River Rapids, or Rafiki's Planet Watch to cool off. And don't forget to drink lots of water.

Go to the thrill rides—Expedition Everest, Dinosaur, and Kali River Rapids—early, before they get too crowded, and try to get a Fastpass.

On the Kilimanjaro Safaris ride, look at the chart over your head. The pictures will show you which animals you're about to see.

Check the Tip Board on Discovery Island to find out how long the wait is for the most popular attractions.

It doesn't really matter what time you get to the safari—the animals are there all day long.

It's Tough to be a Bug! is **very scary** to some kids (especially younger ones and those who don't like the dark). In it, bugs seem to shoot quills and stinky smells, giant spiders dangle from the ceiling, and creepy critters seem to scamper beneath the seats. If you get creeped out during the show, just grab a parent and leave early.

It's fun to see how many animals you can find carved into the Tree of Life and the other buildings on Discovery Island.

Look for your favorite Disney characters in Camp Minnie-Mickey. It's the best place to find them in the park.

Can't find your parents? Ask the closest Disney cast member for help.

Check out the thunder and lightning effects inside the Rainforest Cafe.

 # Attraction Ratings

COOL
(Check It Out)

- The Oasis
- Flights of Wonder
- Affection Section (at Rafiki's Planet Watch)
- TriceraTop Spin
- Pocahontas and Her Forest Friends

REALLY COOL
(Don't Miss)

- The Boneyard playground
- Finding Nemo— The Musical
- Song of the Rain Forest (at Rafiki's Planet Watch)
- Primeval Whirl

THE COOLEST
(See at Least Twice)

- Kilimanjaro Safaris
- Kali River Rapids
- Festival of the Lion King
- Dinosaur
- It's Tough to be a Bug!
- Pangani Forest Exploration Trail
- Maharajah Jungle Trek
- Expedition Everest

Your favorite Animal Kingdom attractions

_____

_____

_____

_____

_____

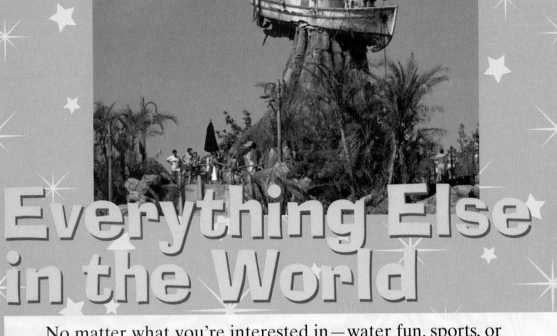

Everything Else in the World

No matter what you're interested in—water fun, sports, or animals—Walt Disney World has enough to make every minute of your vacation a blast. After you visit the theme parks, there's still so much to do. There are water parks, speedy boats to rent, horses to ride, a gigantic arcade, and lots of neat shopping spots.

If you're into sports, check out Disney's Wide World of Sports complex, rent a bike, or try your hand at miniature golf. To test your detective skills, take one of Disney's special scavenger hunts.

In this chapter, you can read up on all the extra activities and find out about hotels and restaurants at Walt Disney World. Then you can help your family decide where to stay, where to eat, and what to do when you're not at the theme parks.

Waters of the World

It's easy to get wet, stay cool, and have fun at Walt Disney World. That's because it's a water wonderland. Choose a water park or take a dip in your hotel pool. If you're under the age of 10, you must have a grown-up with you to enter the water parks.

Typhoon Lagoon

A typhoon is a powerful, windy storm. It dumps huge amounts of rain and sends objects flying through the air. This water park looks like a typhoon hit it. There's even a boat stuck on a mountain top! Of course, a storm didn't really put the boat there—Disney Imagineers did. They also put in pools, waterslides, and a raft ride.

Catch a wave

The big pool here is like a small ocean. It has five-foot waves. That makes body-surfing fun. There are speed slides to try, too. In the mood for a thrill? Try Crush 'n' Gusher. It's like a water roller coaster! For a calmer experience, you can hop into a tube and float along a lazy river. There's also a special area just for younger kids—Ketchakiddee Creek. It has small slides and other games.

Swim with the sharks

Shark Reef is an amazing part of Typhoon Lagoon. It's the home of bonnethead and leopard sharks. And you can swim with them. Don't worry—they are friendly sharks. They don't mind when people swim in their tank. Are you brave enough to swim with the sharks? (There's no age restriction, but you will need to wear a life jacket.)

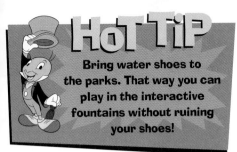

Blizzard Beach

Would you wear a bathing
suit to a snow-covered
mountain? Probably not.
But you should wear one to
Blizzard Beach. It looks like
a place to ski, but it's really a
water park. So don't worry
if you can't ski. Nobody skis
down the mountain here.
They slide!

Reach the peak

Like a real ski resort, all
the action centers around a mountain. In this case, it's Mount
Gushmore. To get to the top, you can take a chairlift. The ride
gives you a great view of the park.

The scariest slide on the mountain is Summit Plummet. It
begins 120 feet in the air, on a platform that looks like a ski
jump. It drops you down a steep slide at about 55 miles per hour.
That's faster than many cars go on the highway.

Slip-sliding away

There are plenty of other ways to slide down the
mountain. Tube slides, body slides, and inner-tube
rides can keep you busy all day long. It's fun to
splash in the wave pool, too.

For preteens, there's Ski Patrol Training Camp,
with its "iceberg" obstacle course, and ropes
for swinging into the water. Tike's Peak is a
special place for younger kids. It has slides and
a snow-castle fountain play area.

READER TIP

"Go to a water park in the
afternoon when it's hot and
crowded at the theme parks.
Then you can return to the
theme park when it cools
down in the evening."

Hailey (age 12)
Saranac, NY

Fort Wilderness

Fort Wilderness is tucked away in a wooded area of Walt Disney World. (It isn't really a fort. It's a campground.) You can stay overnight or just come for a day. There are tennis and volleyball courts, and a marina with lots of boats. You could spend days here and not run out of things to do. If you don't have too much time, you could stop in at the pony farm or rent a boat for a ride around Bay Lake.

Pony Farm

There is a small farm at Fort Wilderness. It's a short walk from Pioneer Hall. There is no charge to visit the farm, but there is a small fee to go for a pony ride. Be sure to bring a grown-up with you. If you don't want to ride a pony, you can still stop by and say hello. Most kids think a visit to the farm is a fun way to spend some time away from the theme parks—especially if they're animal lovers.

More Fort Wilderness Fun

Fort Wilderness offers lots of other things to do. You can rent a canoe for a trip along some canals. Or you can rent a bicycle and explore one of the many trails. At the Tri-Circle-D Ranch, you can see the horses that pull the trolleys in the Magic Kingdom. (They live in a barn near Pioneer Hall.)

Kids over nine years old can take a trail ride on horseback. You can also enjoy a wagon ride, go fishing, or roast marshmallows at a campfire with Chip and Dale.

Sports

Kids who like sports can find plenty of ways to keep active at Walt Disney World. You can rent boats and bikes at one of the resorts, or play miniature golf on one of Disney's themed courses. To see athletes at work, visit Disney's Wide World of Sports complex. Read on to find out how.

Speed Boats

A Sea Raycer is a speedy little motorboat that you can rent. And it delivers big thrills. In most places, if you are 12 or older and at least five feet tall, you can drive one yourself. (At Magic Kingdom resorts, you must be 15 or have a passenger that is a licensed driver.)

These zippy boat rides get very high marks from kids. It goes surprisingly fast and the ride can be bumpy, especially if you drive over a wave caused by another boat. So hang on tight!

You can rent a Sea Raycer at many Disney resorts. The cost is about $25 for a half hour.

Disney's Wide World of Sports Complex

Major sports nuts might enjoy a visit to this complex. It has facilities for every sport you can imagine. The Atlanta Braves baseball team comes here for spring training (in March). The Tampa Bay Buccaneers may hold their training camp here, too. (If so, they'll be here in August.)

You can spend a day watching some amateur events. Tickets to the complex cost about $9 for kids ages 3 through 9, and about $11 for anyone 10 or older. If you want to see a professional game, you have to buy your tickets ahead of time. The prices vary. Have a parent call 407-939-1500 for information.

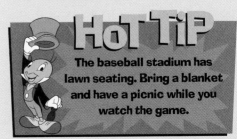

HoT TiP

The baseball stadium has lawn seating. Bring a blanket and have a picnic while you watch the game.

Miniature Golf

Even if you've never held a golf club before, you'll do well at mini golf. It's fun to play, and full of surprises.

Fantasia Gardens

If you have seen the old movie *Fantasia*, you'll know how this miniature golf course got its name. Where else will you find hippos on tiptoe, dancing mushrooms, or xylophone stairs?

The holes are grouped by musical themes. At the Dance of the Hours hole, watch the hippo standing on an alligator. If you hit the ball through the gator's mouth, the hippo dances!

The cost is about $8 to play one round for kids ages 3 through 9, and about $10 for anyone 10 or older.

Disney's Winter Summerland

Sometimes even Santa Claus needs a vacation. Just like you, he picked Walt Disney World as the perfect place to go and have fun.

As the story goes, Santa and his helpers built these mini golf courses as a place to relax and enjoy the sun. That's why one looks like a beach, with sand castles and surfboards on it. But then the elves got homesick, so they built a second course that reminded them of the North Pole. Everything looks like it's covered in snow!

There are even igloos and jolly snowmen, and holes for ice fishing.

For a bit of a challenge, try the summer course. It's a little harder than the winter course. Santa is snoozing at one of the trickiest holes. You have to hit the ball across his lap without waking him up. The winter holes offer fun surprises, too. Get the ball in one of the holes and Mickey himself pops out of a present!

The cost is about $8 to play on one course for kids ages 3 through 9, and about $10 for anyone 10 or older.

Scavenger Hunts

If you are a fan of the tales told by Walt Disney World's shows and rides, you'll probably enjoy these special tours. Each one makes you feel like you are part of the story!

Family Magic Tour

This program is fun for the whole family. Parents and kids can join in a themed scavenger hunt through the Magic Kingdom. Guests search for the answers to different clues that lead to the missing item.

If you go on this two-hour tour, be sure to wear your sneakers—you'll be doing lots of walking! The cost is about $27 for everyone age 3 and over. Parents should call 407-WDW-TOUR (939-8687) to make reservations.

Pirate Adventure

Did you know that there is a pirate's treasure buried near the Magic Kingdom? It's said to be hidden somewhere in the Seven Seas lagoon. A few times a week an expedition just for kids sails out from the Grand Floridian in search of it.

Do you think you are up to the challenge? The captain of the ship will give you a map and a series of puzzling clues to help you on your way. During the journey, kids get to eat a light lunch. You have two hours to find the treasure. And if you do, it's yours to keep! This program is for kids ages 4 to 10. Cost is about $28 per child.

Parents should call 407-939-3463 for reservations.

Who am I?

- Pooh is my pal.
- I'm yellow.
- My name starts with "R."

Answer: Rabbit

Downtown Disney

What has interesting shops and restaurants, movies, dance spots, boats to rent, and much more? Downtown Disney! It has three sections: the West Side, Pleasure Island, and the Marketplace. Pleasure Island isn't for kids, but the West Side and Marketplace have plenty of cool places for you to explore.

The West Side

This is the newest section of Downtown Disney. It has places to shop, eat, and catch a movie, plus DisneyQuest (read all about it on the next page).

There's even an exciting show by Cirque du Soleil (pronounced: *serk due so-LAY*). It's performed in a building that looks like a giant circus tent—but this show's not like an ordinary circus! You won't see a ringmaster or wild animals. Instead, there are gymnasts and acrobats dressed in colorful costumes. They twist their bodies and dance in unusual ways. Parents can buy tickets by calling 407-939-7600 or visiting *disneyworld.com*.

The Marketplace

Searching for that perfect souvenir? The best place to look is in the Marketplace. There are dozens of shops to browse in. You can also make a wacky creation at the Lego Imagination Center. One store that shouldn't be missed is called World of Disney. It's the biggest Disney store in the world.

Hidden Mickey Alert!

Some of the Marketplace's dancing water fountains form the shape of you-know-who!

DisneyQuest

This place is probably bigger than any arcade you've ever seen. It's filled from top to bottom with every interactive game imaginable. It might not be open during your visit, so have your parents call to check (407-WDW-DISNEY).

Pick a zone

DisneyQuest is separated into four different areas called "zones." In the **Explore Zone** you can visit faraway places on virtual-reality adventures. You might go on a pirate voyage, take a trip on Aladdin's magic carpet, or ride the rapids on a prehistoric jungle cruise.

The center of the **Score Zone** is a gigantic pinball game called Mighty Ducks Pinball Slam. In it, the people are giant joysticks! This zone is also the place to find all different kinds of brand-new games.

Future Imagineers will love the **Create Zone**. Here you can take a short animation class, try computer painting, or have stickers made out of your photo. You can also design your own roller coaster and then ride it on CyberSpace Mountain, a virtual-reality ride that goes upside down and twists all around. (Don't do this right after you eat!)

In the **Replay Zone** you get prizes for the points you earn on some of the games (these games cost extra). Choose from favorites like Skee Ball and Whack an Alien. There's also a room full of video games that were popular more than ten years ago. Ask your parents if they remember any of them!

Take a break

There is so much to choose from! Kids all agree that you could spend a few hours playing here.

Once you're inside (and paid your admission fee), you won't have to pay to play games. But be sure to give others a chance to enjoy your favorites, too!

DisneyQuest is a good place to spend time when the weather's really hot or rainy. Or if you just love arcades.

READER TIP

"Expect a long line for CyberSpace Mountain at DisneyQuest. It's very popular!"

Veronica (age 11)
Bloomington, IN

Walt Disney World Resorts

There are more than 20 different resorts on Walt Disney World property. There are so many hotel rooms that you could stay in a different one every night for 55 years!

Just like the rides at the parks, each of the resorts has its own special theme. And all of the resorts are fun to stay at. But they are fun to visit, too. So if you have time, you might want to stop by some of them—to have a meal or just to enjoy the atmosphere.

Resorts near the
Magic Kingdom

CONTEMPORARY

This was the first Walt Disney World hotel. It looked very modern when it was built in 1971 (that's how it got its name). When it opened, it had a talking elevator and a monorail station right in the middle of it. It still has the monorail today, plus an arcade and Chef Mickey's—one of the best character restaurants in all of Walt Disney World.

Contemporary Tip
In the center of the resort is a mural that's 90 feet tall. There are colorful pictures of children and animals all over it. One of the goats has five legs. See how long it takes you to spot him!

FORT WILDERNESS

Stay in your family camper or rent a cabin at this pretty wooded campground. This resort has many activities. You can go for a hayride, visit a pony farm, or take a trip through the woods on a horse. At night, Chip and Dale sometimes roast marshmallows by a campfire. This is also home to a popular dinner show called the Hoop-Dee-Doo Musical Revue.

Fort Wilderness Tip
There are lots of trees in the woods of Fort Wilderness. But there's only one that's famous. It's called the Lawn Mower Tree. You'll know why when you find it!

GRAND FLORIDIAN

This elegant hotel looks like a huge mansion from the early 1900s. At first, it seems to be designed for grown-ups, but it's also fun for kids. There are special activities, like face painting and storytelling. At night you can sit in a big, comfy chair and listen to an old-fashioned band play in the main building. There is also a pretty pool with roses all around it. The monorail has a station here, too.

Grand Floridian Tip
At Christmas-time, the Grand Floridian lobby is home to a giant gingerbread house. It's made of real gingerbread — and so big that people can actually go inside!

The Monorail

The monorail connects the Magic Kingdom with the **Contemporary**, **Polynesian**, and **Grand Floridian** resorts. It's also the best way to get from the Magic Kingdom to Epcot or the Transportation and Ticket Center. At some stations, a family can sit up front with the driver. Ask a cast member if you can take a turn.

Everything Else in the World

POLYNESIAN

The plants and trees at this hotel make it look like a tropical island. The greenery and waterfalls in the main building make the setting seem real even when you're indoors. There's a pool that looks like a volcano that's about to erupt, and a beautiful beach to relax on. The monorail also stops here.

Polynesian Tip
Join the Big Kahuna in welcoming the night at the weekend torch-lighting ceremonies. Before the torches are lit, there is a terrific flame-twirling act.

WILDERNESS LODGE

With its log columns and totem poles, this hotel looks like a national park from the American Northwest. The fireplaces and rocking chairs in the main building make you feel right at home. Outside, there's an erupting geyser and a pool that looks like it's part of a hot spring. There are so many Hidden Mickeys here that there's even a tour and contest to see how many you can find!

Wilderness Lodge Tip
Look for the "Proterozoic Fossils and Minerals" display. It's a rock key to the strata of the giant Grand Canyon fireplace in the main lobby.

Everything Else in the World

BOARDWALK

This hotel is designed to look like Atlantic City, New Jersey, once did. Just like on an old-fashioned boardwalk, there are games and snack stands here for everyone to enjoy. You can rent a special bicycle built for four, or swim in a pool that looks like an amusement park.

BoardWalk Tip

Look for a crystal globe under a chandelier in the main building. It's actually a Disney time capsule that will be opened on Walt Disney World's 50th anniversary.

READER TIP

"The TVs in Disney hotel rooms have a channel that's all about Disney World. Don't miss it!"

Nicholas (age 9)
Mount Pleasant, SC

PORT ORLEANS RIVERSIDE

This hotel used to be called Dixie Landings. The name has changed, but the hotel's buildings still look like mansions and country homes from the Old South. The food court is designed after a cotton mill and it has a real waterwheel that's 30 feet tall.

Riverside Tip

If you like to fish, head down to the Ol' Fishin' Hole. The resort has poles to rent and worms to buy.

CARIBBEAN BEACH

Happy and colorful, this hotel looks like resorts on Caribbean islands. You can have fun in the sun all day at its beaches, pools, and playgrounds.

Caribbean Beach Tip

Don't worry about packing a sand bucket or shovel—the kids' meals at the food court come with them!

PORT ORLEANS FRENCH QUARTER

The special details at this hotel make it look like New Orleans, Louisiana. There's a long river, and a fun pool with a curving dragon waterslide.

French Quarter Tip

After taking a dip in the French Quarter pool, you might want to check out the pool at Port Orleans Riverside. You can get there by walking or taking a Walt Disney World bus. Be sure to take your parents with you!

OLD KEY WEST

The town houses that make up this resort have all the comforts of home. The palm trees and sunny design make it a very warm and welcoming place. And the pool has an awesome slide!

Old Key West Tip
Kids ages 5 through 12 can sign up for an Un-Birthday Party. You'll enjoy the games and the cupcake that come with it.

POP CENTURY RESORT

The twentieth century might be over, but it's hard to forget at this humongous hotel. Giant icons (like cell phones and jukeboxes) decorate the buildings. The hotel pays tribute to each decade from the 1950s to the 1990s.

Pop Century Tip
On hot days, cool off by splashing around in the hotel's interactive fountains.

SWAN AND DOLPHIN

You can't miss the dolphin and swan statues that sit on top of these two hotels—they're gigantic. Together the hotels have lots to do and many restaurants. You can walk to Epcot, the Disney-MGM Studios, and the BoardWalk resort from both hotels.

Swan and Dolphin Tip
There are 250 swan and dolphin statues at this resort. Some are big, but some are very small. See how many you can spot.

SARATOGA SPRINGS RESORT & SPA

This is the newest hotel at Walt Disney World. It's designed to look like upstate New York in the late 1800s. There are lots of pretty gardens to look at. But the best views come from a special lakeside spot. From there you can see the lights of Downtown Disney.

Saratoga Springs Tip
The pool area has a special water-spray play area with lots of squirting fountains. It's just for kids!

YACHT AND BEACH CLUB

These two connected hotels are designed after the homes near the beaches of Massachusetts. Even the pool makes you feel like you're at the beach—the bottom of it is covered with real sand!

Yacht and Beach Club Tip
Be sure to bring your sneakers. One of the best parts about staying here is that you can walk to Epcot, the Disney-MGM Studios, and BoardWalk.

READER TIP
"If you stay at a Disney hotel, make sure to ask for a wake-up call. It's usually Mickey or one of his friends."

Raquel (age 7)
Miami, FL

Resorts near
Animal Kingdom

READER TIP

"If you get a chance, you should go swimming at your hotel's pool at night. It's lots of fun!"

Laura (age 11)
Alexandria, VA

ALL-STAR RESORTS

There are three All-Star resorts, and each of them has its own theme— sports, music, or movies. It's easy to tell which All-Star you're at, because they have giant icons that are even bigger than the buildings. At All-Star Music, look for the big cowboy boots. A huge football helmet shows you you're at All-Star Sports. And when you see a 38-foot-tall Buzz Lightyear, there's no doubt you're at All-Star Movies.

All-Star Tip

There are a whole lot of Hidden Mickeys to hunt for. Start your search at the main statue in each of the resorts.

CORONADO SPRINGS

The land at this hotel looks like parts of the southwestern U.S. and Mexico. The buildings are the color of clay. There's a pool that looks like an ancient pyramid, with a slide that passes under a spitting jaguar. Beside it is a sandbox with ancient treasures waiting to be uncovered.

Coronado Springs Tip

Some of the food at the restaurant here might be new to you. If you don't like Mexican food, be sure to order from the kids' menu.

Disney Cruise Line

Set sail on a Disney ship with Mickey and his friends. You could visit Walt Disney World for a few days and then cruise to the Caribbean. There you can explore Disney's private island, Castaway Cay. Each ship has special activity areas, pools, and programs just for kids, so you can do your own thing while your parents relax.

ANIMAL KINGDOM LODGE

Creatures like giraffes, zebras, gazelles, and beautiful birds live near this hotel. The trees and animals make it seem like the resort is set in a real African savanna. A giant mud fireplace and thatched ceilings add to the feeling that you are at a big campsite in Africa.

Animal Kingdom Lodge Tip

Almost all of the rooms have excellent views of the animals. But if you want an even closer look, remember to bring a pair of binoculars from home.

Restaurants

Eating at Walt Disney World can be as much fun as riding Splash Mountain (well, almost as much fun!). Here are our suggestions for the best spots in each theme park to head to for your favorite foods.

Magic Kingdom
Best Places for Favorite Foods

Candy and crispie treats . . . . .Main Street Confectionery

Chicken fingers . . . . .Crystal Palace

Chili . . . . .Pecos Bill Cafe

Chocolate-chip cookies . . . . Main Street Bakery

Fruit . . . . .Liberty Square Market

Hamburgers . . . . Pecos Bill Cafe

Hot dogs . . . . Casey's Corner

Ice cream . . . . .Plaza Ice Cream Parlor

Macaroni and cheese . . . . Columbia Harbour House

Pizza . . . . .Pinocchio Village Haus

Pretzels . . . . .Fantasyland Pretzel Stand

Turkey legs . . . . Lunching Pad at Rockettower Plaza

Veggie burgers .Cosmic Ray's Starlight Cafe

Epcot
Best Places for Favorite Foods

Cookies . . . . .Kringla Bakeri Og Kafe (in Norway)

Egg rolls . . . . .Lotus Blossom Cafe (in China)

Fruit . . . . Sunshine Seasons (in The Land)

Gummy bears .Süssigkeiten (in Germany)

Hamburgers . . . . Electric Umbrella (in Innoventions)

Ice cream . . . . Refreshment Cool Post (World Showcase,
between China and Germany)

Macaroni and cheese . . . . .Electric Umbrella (in Future World)

Pastries . . . . Boulangerie Patisserie (in France)

Peanut butter and jelly sandwiches . . . Sunshine Seasons (in The Land)

Sausage . . . . Sommerfest (in Germany)

Soft pretzels . . . . Sommerfest (in Germany)

Spaghetti . . . . .Italian restaurant (in Italy)

Tacos . . . . .Cantina de San Angel (in Mexico)

Disney-MGM Studios
Best Places for Favorite Foods

Everything Else in the World

HoT TiP

Most restaurants have special menus for kids. Just ask!

Disney's Animal Kingdom
Best Places for Favorite Foods

Barbecued ribs . . . . Flame Tree Barbecue
Candy . . . . Chester and Hester's Dinosaur Treasures
Chicken nuggets and fries . . . . Restaurantosaurus
Cookies . . . . Kusafiri Coffee Shop & Bakery
Fruit . . . . Harambe Fruit Market
Grilled cheese . . . . Rainforest Cafe
Hamburgers . . . . .Restaurantosaurus
Hot dogs . . . . Restaurantosaurus
Ice cream . . . . Tamu Tamu Refreshments
Pizza . . . . Pizzafari
Turkey legs . . . . Safari Turkey Cart
Veggie burgers . . . . Rainforest Cafe

Eating with the Characters

Kids of all ages enjoy eating with the characters. It's one of the best ways to see your favorite Disney stars. They will come right up to your table to meet you. Bring a camera because the characters are also happy to pose for photos. And don't forget your pen so you can collect some autographs!

Each of the theme parks has at least one restaurant that invites the characters over. Many of the resorts have character meals, too. They are very popular, so no matter which restaurant your family chooses, it's a good idea to make reservations ahead of time. Ask a parent to call 407-WDW-DINE (939-3463).

Character meals aren't just fun because you get to see the characters. They're special because the food is served in a special way. Depending on which restaurant you choose, the meal will either be presented in a buffet or family style. Picky eaters may prefer one of the buffets—with so much to choose from, you're sure to find something you like!

Dinner Shows

Hoop-Dee-Doo Musical Revue
Entertainers sing, dance, and tell jokes while you chow down on chicken, ribs, and corn. The jokes are silly, but everyone always has a good time. That's probably why the Hoop-Dee-Doo is the most popular dinner show in Walt Disney World!

Mickey's Backyard Barbecue
Mickey's having a barbecue, and you are welcome to join the fun. You can eat all the chicken, hot dogs, barbecued ribs, and dessert you want, while a live band plays country music. There's also a show for kids, games, and dancing with the Disney characters.

The Spirit of Aloha
Aloha! That means "hello" (and "good-bye") in Hawaiian. You'll hear it a lot at this show. Performers do the hula and other Hawaiian dances, while servers dish out Polynesian food.

Reservations for all of these shows should be made before you arrive at Walt Disney World. Your parents can call 407-WDW-DINE (939-3463).

Magical Memories

The fun doesn't have to end when your vacation does. Use these pages to preserve your Disney memories.

These are the people I vacationed with:

I arrived at Walt Disney World on:
_____
(month/day/year)
I stayed for _____ days.

My first day at Walt Disney World I went to:

I traveled to Walt Disney World by:

[ ] car
[ ] plane
[ ] bus
[ ] boat
[ ] train

The name of our hotel was:

I went on this ride first:

My usual bedtime is _____ o'clock.

During my trip, the latest I went to bed was _____ o'clock.

The earliest I woke up was _____ o'clock.

Draw your favorite Disney character here!

The weather at Walt Disney World was:

[ ] sunny
[ ] rainy
[ ] windy
[ ] chilly
[ ] snowy

This attraction wasn't what I expected:

It surprised me because it was:

The scariest ride I went on was:

My favorite ride was:

I went on it _____ times.

Tape a used Walt Disney World ticket here!

If I were an Imagineer, this is the ride I would design:

My least favorite ride was:

I didn't like it because it was:

Magical Memories

The best Disney theme park was:

[ ] Magic Kingdom
[ ] Epcot
[ ] Disney-MGM Studios
[ ] Disney's Animal Kingdom

Vacations aren't just fun, they're educational, too! One thing that I learned at Walt Disney World is:

My favorite restaurant was:

I ate:

Building a theme park was Walt Disney's dream. What's your dream?

The funniest thing that happened at Walt Disney World was:

Paste a Walt Disney World vacation photo here!

I found _____ Hidden Mickeys.

The best
Walt Disney World
snack is:

I met _____ characters
during my vacation.

The first character I saw was:

Tape the corner
of a
Walt Disney World
napkin here!

Tape a
Walt Disney World
receipt here!

It's fun to remember a vacation with souvenirs.
One souvenir I brought back is:

My favorite character is:

Someday, I'll go back to Walt Disney World.
The first thing I'll do when I get there is:

Autographs

Disney characters love to sign autographs.
Bring a pen and ask them to sign these pages for you!

Autographs